STAR WARS

THE VISUAL DICTIONARY

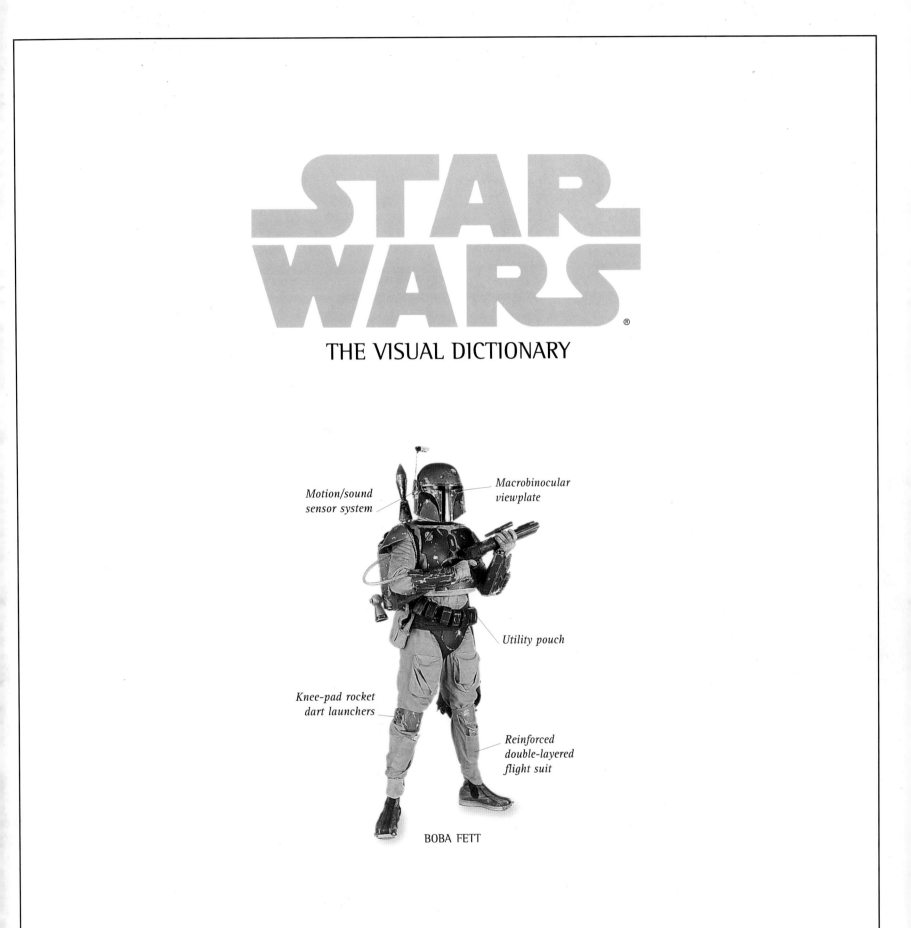

Motion/sound
sensor system

Macrobinocular
viewplate

Utility pouch

Knee-pad rocket
dart launchers

Reinforced
double-layered
flight suit

BOBA FETT

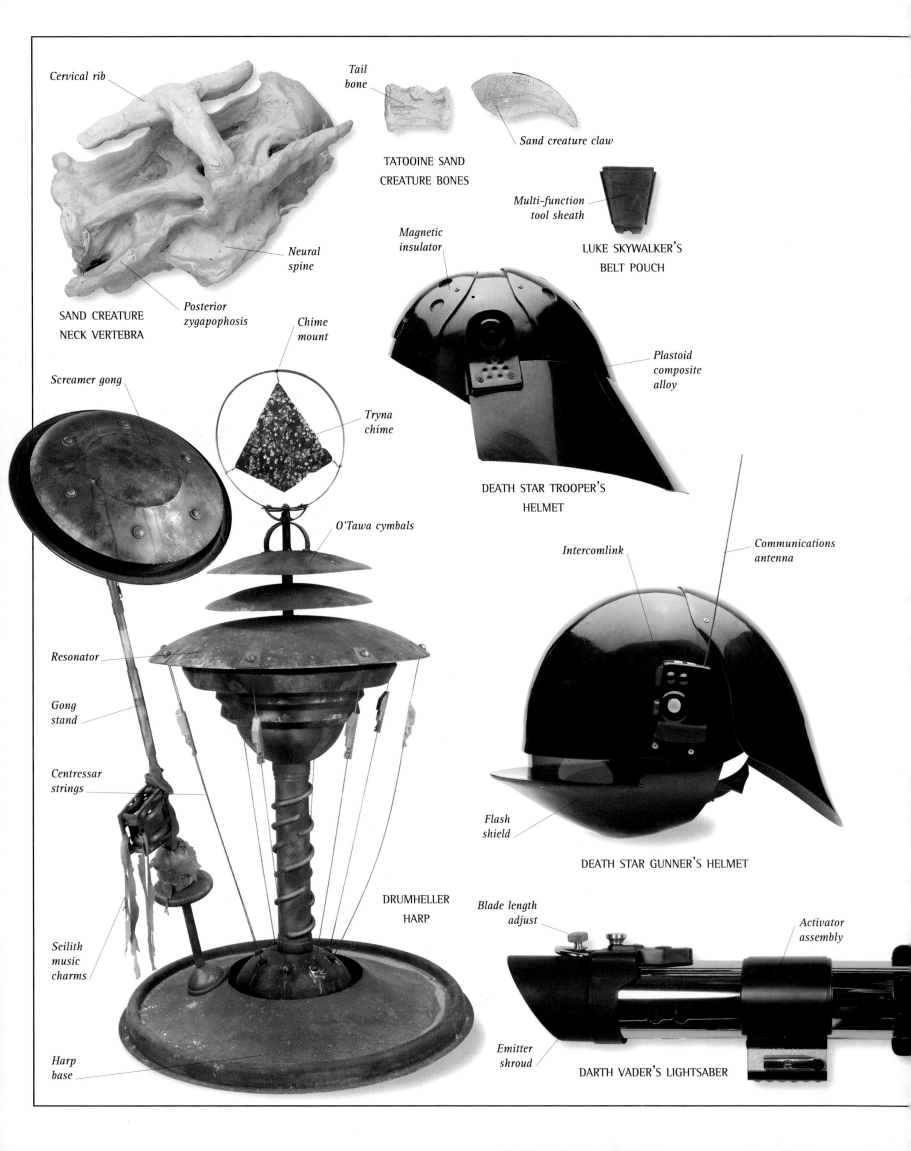

Cervical rib

Tail bone

Sand creature claw

TATOOINE SAND
CREATURE BONES

Magnetic insulator

Multi-function tool sheath

LUKE SKYWALKER'S
BELT POUCH

Neural spine

Posterior zygapophosis

SAND CREATURE
NECK VERTEBRA

Chime mount

Screamer gong

Tryna chime

Plastoid composite alloy

DEATH STAR TROOPER'S
HELMET

O'Tawa cymbals

Communications antenna

Intercomlink

Resonator

Gong stand

Centressar strings

Flash shield

DEATH STAR GUNNER'S HELMET

DRUMHELLER
HARP

Seilith music charms

Blade length adjust

Activator assembly

Harp base

Emitter shroud

DARTH VADER'S LIGHTSABER

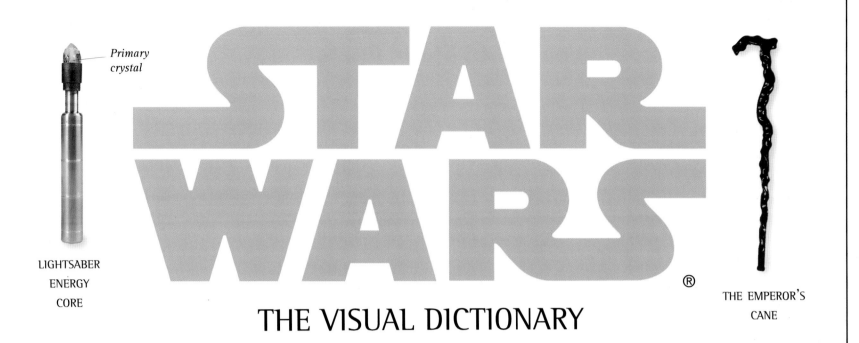

Primary
crystal

LIGHTSABER
ENERGY
CORE

THE EMPEROR'S
CANE

STAR WARS®

THE VISUAL DICTIONARY

Written by
DAVID WEST REYNOLDS

Special Fabrications by
DON BIES & NELSON HALL

New Photography by
ALEXANDER IVANOV

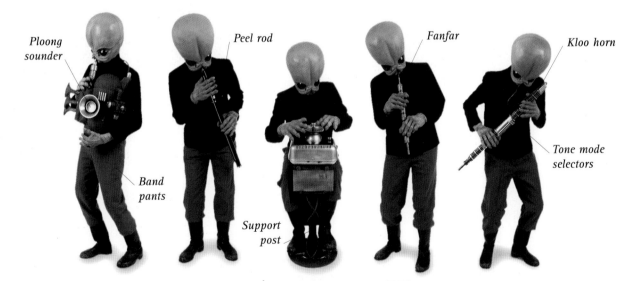

Ploong
sounder

Peel rod

Fanfar

Kloo horn

Band
pants

Support
post

Tone mode
selectors

FIGRIN D'AN AND THE MODAL NODES

Handgrip

DK PUBLISHING, INC.

LUKE SKYWALKER'S
BELT POUCH

Contents

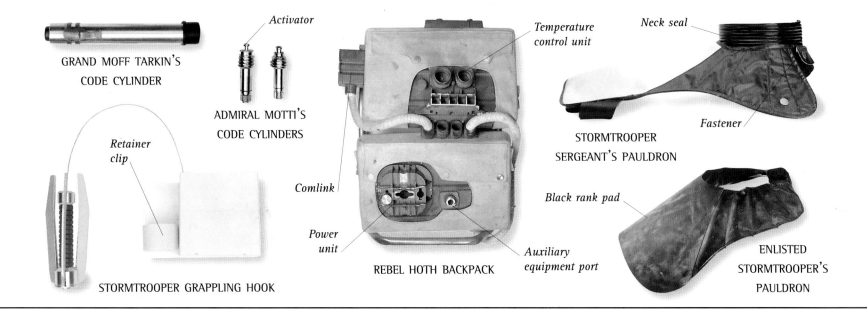

GRAND MOFF TARKIN'S
CODE CYLINDER

Activator

ADMIRAL MOTTI'S
CODE CYLINDERS

Retainer
clip

STORMTROOPER GRAPPLING HOOK

Temperature
control unit

Comlink

Power
unit

Auxiliary
equipment port

REBEL HOTH BACKPACK

Neck seal

Fastener

STORMTROOPER
SERGEANT'S PAULDRON

Black rank pad

ENLISTED
STORMTROOPER'S
PAULDRON

Introduction

THE FANTASY WORLD of the *Star Wars* trilogy has come to take on a curious feeling of reality. Created for movies, the clothing, weapons, technology, and other items appearing in this Visual Dictionary feature the nicks and dents of longtime use, the look of no-nonsense functionality, and the convincing detail of actual objects. The characters, creatures, and droids of *Star Wars* were given extensive back-stories and personal histories that bring them to their points of adventure on the screen. It is the extraordinarily rich conception of *Star Wars* and its trappings that makes the fantasy seem so real. The devoted labors of many inspired artists and performers wrought a universe so detailed that we can hold it up to intense scrutiny, always discovering new subtleties in the marvellous tapestry. Herein you will find the tangible elements of the *Star Wars* saga explained in detail and presented with clarity as never before. Here you may come very close to touching all this imaginary reality for yourself. You hold in your hands a guidebook and a passport to a place where the blaster bolts smell of ozone and the rock canyons of Tatooine hide mysterious eyes in the dark. Join us.

Welcome to the world of *Star Wars*.

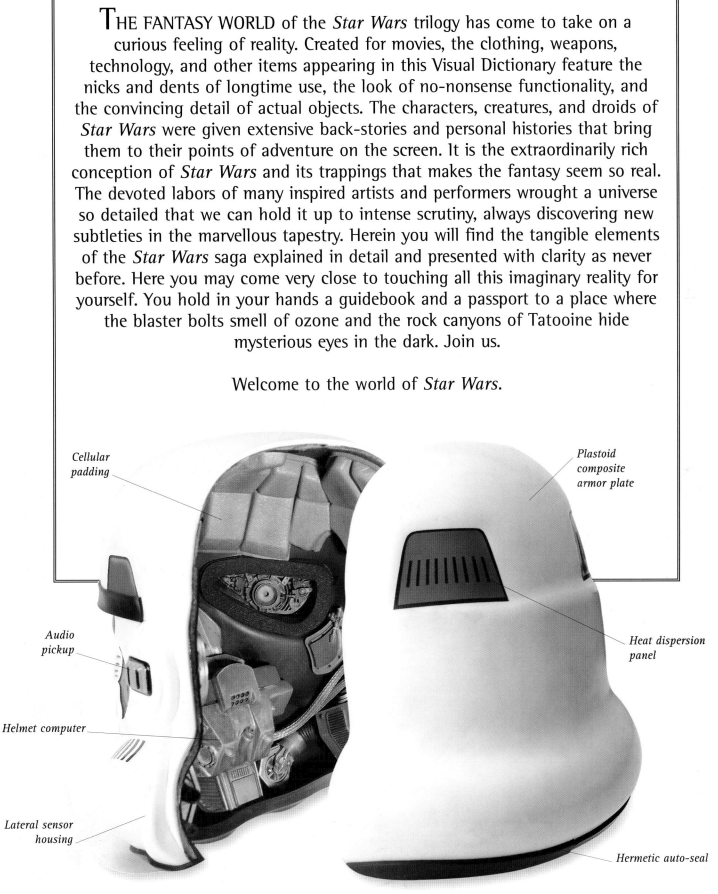

Cellular padding

Plastoid composite armor plate

Audio pickup

Helmet computer

Heat dispersion panel

Lateral sensor housing

Hermetic auto-seal

CUT-AWAY STORMTROOPER HELMET

Special Technology

FOR THOUSANDS OF YEARS high technology has existed throughout the galaxy, ebbing and flowing with the rise and fall of civilizations. The development of technology has taken many different and uneven paths, and what is a natural extension to one culture may be overlooked by another for ages. Traditional technology such as the Jedi lightsaber may remain constant for centuries. Alternatively, military pressures may bring new innovations in areas which have remained unchanged for millennia. As cultures meet and interact, advanced devices fall into the hands of otherwise primitive groups, and many creatures use technology of which they have no real understanding.

Reinforced stock

ION BLASTERS
Complex electronic components can be disrupted by ion blasts. Ion cannons can disable spacecraft without damaging them, while custom-built Jawa ionization blasters stun droids in the same way.

OBI-WAN KENOBI'S LIGHTSABER

LUKE SKYWALKER'S SECOND LIGHTSABER

DARTH VADER'S LIGHTSABER

Lightsaber designs often relate to personal histories. Darth Vader's lightsaber looks much like the one he used as a Jedi learner, only darker. Luke Skywalker's lightsaber, on the other hand, follows the type used by Luke's mentor Ben Kenobi.

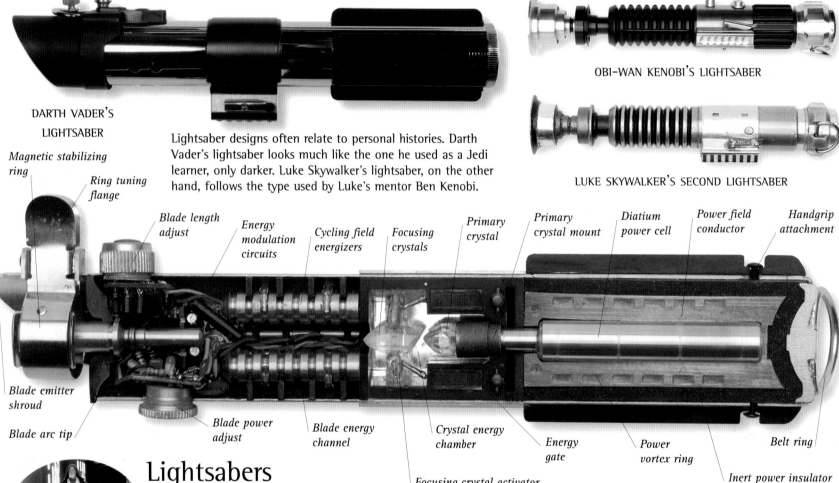

Magnetic stabilizing ring

Ring tuning flange

Blade length adjust

Energy modulation circuits

Cycling field energizers

Focusing crystals

Primary crystal

Primary crystal mount

Diatium power cell

Power field conductor

Handgrip attachment

Blade emitter shroud

Blade arc tip

Blade power adjust

Blade energy channel

Crystal energy chamber

Focusing crystal activator

Energy gate

Power vortex ring

Inert power insulator

Belt ring

Lightsabers

Lightsabers tend to follow a similar basic structure, although many are very individualized by their Jedi builders. While the pure energy blade has no mass, the electromagnetically generated arc wave creates a strong gyroscopic effect that makes the lightsaber a distinct challenge to handle. Operating on the complex principle of tightly controlled arc-wave energy, it requires focusing elements made from naturally-occurring crystals that cannot be synthesized. A lightsaber must be assembled by hand, as there is no exact formula for the crucial alignment of the irregular crystals. The slightest misalignment will cause the weapon to detonate on activation.

Luke Skywalker and Darth Vader duel in Cloud City

The legendary lightsaber is the ancient traditional weapon of the Jedi Knight, guardians of justice for so many generations. Building a working lightsaber is one of the threshold tests for Jedi initiates: accomplishing the impossibly fine alignment task proves their Force sensitivity.

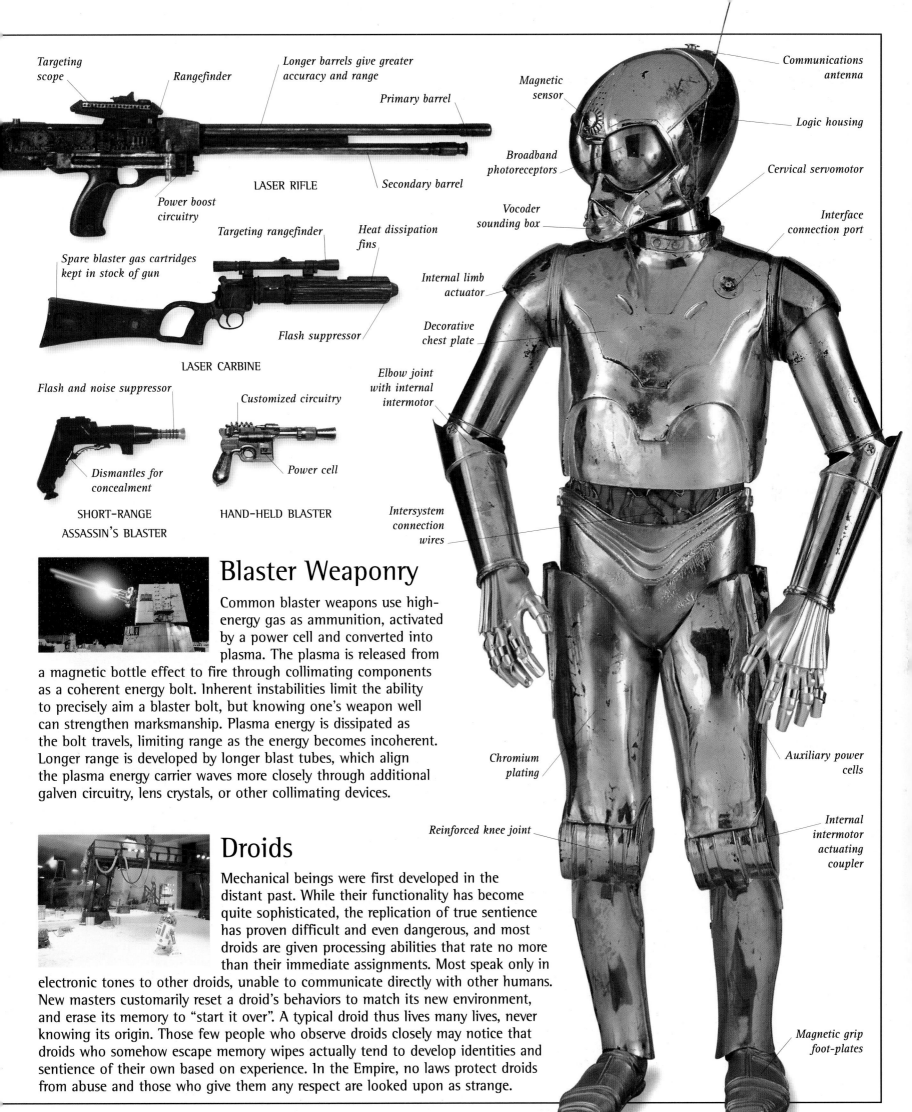

Targeting scope

Rangefinder

Longer barrels give greater accuracy and range

Primary barrel

Power boost circuitry

Secondary barrel

LASER RIFLE

Spare blaster gas cartridges kept in stock of gun

Targeting rangefinder

Heat dissipation fins

Flash suppressor

LASER CARBINE

Flash and noise suppressor

Customized circuitry

Dismantles for concealment

Power cell

SHORT-RANGE ASSASSIN'S BLASTER

HAND-HELD BLASTER

Communications antenna

Magnetic sensor

Logic housing

Broadband photoreceptors

Cervical servomotor

Vocoder sounding box

Interface connection port

Internal limb actuator

Decorative chest plate

Elbow joint with internal intermotor

Intersystem connection wires

Chromium plating

Auxiliary power cells

Reinforced knee joint

Internal intermotor actuating coupler

Magnetic grip foot-plates

Blaster Weaponry

Common blaster weapons use high-energy gas as ammunition, activated by a power cell and converted into plasma. The plasma is released from a magnetic bottle effect to fire through collimating components as a coherent energy bolt. Inherent instabilities limit the ability to precisely aim a blaster bolt, but knowing one's weapon well can strengthen marksmanship. Plasma energy is dissipated as the bolt travels, limiting range as the energy becomes incoherent. Longer range is developed by longer blast tubes, which align the plasma energy carrier waves more closely through additional galven circuitry, lens crystals, or other collimating devices.

Droids

Mechanical beings were first developed in the distant past. While their functionality has become quite sophisticated, the replication of true sentience has proven difficult and even dangerous, and most droids are given processing abilities that rate no more than their immediate assignments. Most speak only in electronic tones to other droids, unable to communicate directly with other humans. New masters customarily reset a droid's behaviors to match its new environment, and erase its memory to "start it over". A typical droid thus lives many lives, never knowing its origin. Those few people who observe droids closely may notice that droids who somehow escape memory wipes actually tend to develop identities and sentience of their own based on experience. In the Empire, no laws protect droids from abuse and those who give them any respect are looked upon as strange.

Luke Skywalker

LUKE AND BIGGS DARKLIGHTER

A YOUNG FARMBOY living on the remote desert planet Tatooine, Luke Skywalker yearns to escape the dull routine of his daily chores on his uncle's moisture farm. Luke dreams of becoming a space pilot, but is torn between his desire to enroll in the Academy and his loyalty to his uncle and aunt, who need him on the farm. When Luke discovers a cryptic secret message hidden in one of his new droids, he sets out on a quest and is catapulted into a world of adventure which will at last fulfill his true destiny.

Luke's home is mostly underground, to escape the heat of Tatooine's twin suns. Tunnels connect the main courtyard to the hangar well and the covered garage.

Garage roof   Entrance dome   Salt flats   Courtyard

Cistern cap   Moisture vaporator extracts water vapor from air   Fusion generator supply tanks

Toshi power station in the small town of Anchorhead offers a place for Luke to escape the farm and spend time with his friends – talking, playing electronically-assisted pool, or tinkering with his landspeeder or skyhopper.

Luke first encounters part of the hidden truth about his father when Ben Kenobi gives him his father's Jedi lightsaber. In Luke's hands it flares to life again for the first time in many years.

Droid caller

Tool pouch

Utility belt

Tatooine farm tunic

Light pants

Sandproof leg bindings

Grip soles

Blade stabilizing ring

Blade length adjust

Quick recharge plug

Anakin Skywalker's lightsaber

Activation matrix

AUNT BERU LARS

UNCLE OWEN LARS

Power cell   Handgrip

Lightsaber

A gift from another era, Luke's lightsaber is the legacy of his father Anakin, a former Jedi Knight of the Old Republic and a warrior who fought in the Clone Wars. A symbol of Luke's destiny, the lightsaber is unlike any other weapon. Luke has a natural ability with the saber and begins to learn rapidly from his mentor Ben Kenobi.

Pitting from desert sand and gravel

Air circulation grille over cooling intakes and exhaust

Model includes decor and enhanced components Luke hopes to get when he can afford them

Emblem Luke would like to add

Pneumatic projectile gun for blasting womp rats

Display base

Luke's macrobinoculars provide electronic zoom and image enhancement capability, as well as target range and bearing

Luke owns a suborbital T-16 skyhopper (his own model of it is shown above), which he races through the narrow ravines of Beggar's Canyon with his friends, blasting womp rat dens in sheltered hollows. Having narrowly made it through both Diablo Cut and the Stone Needle, Luke has proven himself an excellent pilot. He cannot search for R2-D2 in the skyhopper because his uncle has grounded him for reckless flying.

While working on a vaporator, Luke uses his macrobinoculars to observe a space battle between two ships far overhead.

The kitchen of the Lars home is typical of moisture farms, with many moisture-saving devices. The kitchen passage leads up to the dining room, which opens onto the main courtyard.

R2-D2 appears on the landspeeder scanner

LANDSPEEDER SCANNER

Luke's Landspeeder

Luke's X-34 landspeeder hovers above the ground, suspended by low-power repulsorlifts which keep the craft floating even when parked. Three turbines boost the repulsor drive effect and jet the 'speeder across the wide open spaces of the desert. The windshield can be closed to a sealed bubble, but Luke hasn't been able to fix the back half, so he keeps the cockpit open.

Crash damage

Repulsor drive generators

LANDSPEEDER – SIDE AND REAR

Thrust turbine vent

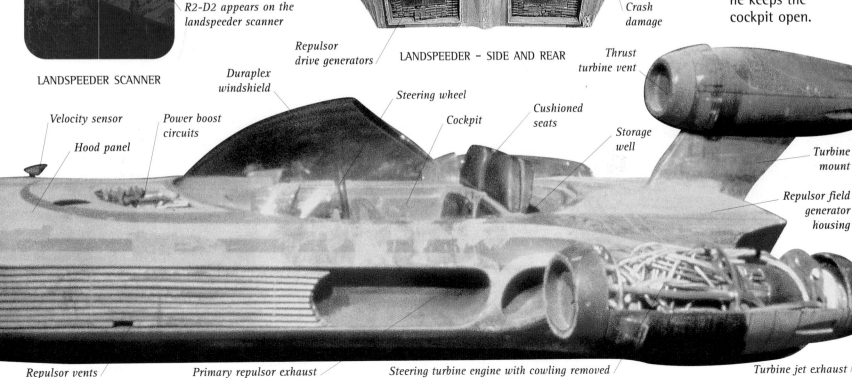

Velocity sensor

Hood panel

Power boost circuits

Duraplex windshield

Steering wheel

Cockpit

Cushioned seats

Storage well

Turbine mount

Repulsor field generator housing

Repulsor vents

Primary repulsor exhaust

Steering turbine engine with cowling removed

Turbine jet exhaust

Skywalker: Pilot and Jedi

LUKE SKYWALKER first climbs into the cockpit of an X-wing starfighter to fly as "Red Five" in the attack on the first Death Star. Fighting for the Alliance in the years afterward, Luke takes his X-wing and other craft into battle and adventure against space pirates and Imperial ships, bringing victories for the hard-pressed Rebels and becoming one of their most innovative leaders. His Force abilities are awakened by Master Yoda and, over the years, Luke grows towards the moment when he will become a Jedi Knight at last.

Chest pack straps

Pressurized g-suit

Data cylinders

Safe passage documents for downed pilots

Flak vest

Life support unit

Insulated helmet

Alliance symbol

Flight gauntlets

Wrist seals

Gear harness

Equipment pocket

Signal flares

Flight boots

Positive-grip soles

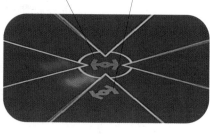

Strike zone

TIE fighter

While not as advanced as Imperial targeting equipment, the X-wing targeting display still provides confirmation of targets within the strike zone of the four oversized long-range laser cannons.

T-65 X-wing

X-wing fighters include a socket for an astromech droid, which handles in-flight maintenance and repairs. The X-wing fighter carries a small payload of proton torpedoes in addition to its laser cannons, but the torpedoes are expensive ordnance in short supply for the Alliance and Luke goes into battle against the Death Star with only a single pair.

Astromech droid

Wings open to X configuration for combat

Long-range laser cannons

Targeting computer signal to fire

Simulation of proton torpedo entering the small thermal exhaust port that is the Rebels' target

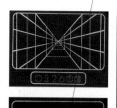

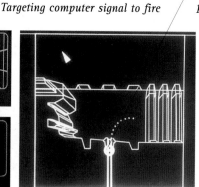

X-WING TARGETING COMPUTER READOUTS

The stolen Death Star plans allow the Rebel leaders to simulate the effects of different kinds of attacks on the battle station.

The target exhaust shaft leads straight to the hypermatter reactor deep within the core of the Death Star. Luke takes his critical shot using the Force, triumphantly destroying the entire gigantic battle station.

Harpoon gun — *Reinforced cockpit frame*

Power convertors

Added armor plate

Wedge shape helps snowspeeders operate easily in strong winds

Snowspeeder

Luke helped the Alliance acquire its squadron of defense speeder craft, equipped with armor plating and heavy-duty blaster cannons. Laboriously modified to operate in the frozen temperatures of Hoth, the snowspeeders have no defensive shields and must rely on agility and speed in battle. Luke, as a wing commander, leads the Rogue Squadron of snowspeeders against the Imperial Blizzard Force AT-ATs.

Luke's bravery takes him into situations which wipe out his equipment, but he never gives up. Blasted from the sky on Hoth, Luke struggles out of his cockpit before the snowspeeder is crushed by an AT-AT.

Jedi Knight

Having faced the challenge of his father's identity, Luke develops his abilities with the Force according to the teachings of his mentors Ben Kenobi and Yoda. Though he walks his path alone and without fellow initiates, Luke strives to fulfill his destiny and become a Jedi. Returning to Dagobah, he learns from Yoda that he has almost achieved that noble level at last. Centering his determination, Luke moves on to face the darkest challenges of the Emperor and Darth Vader, holding in his heart the galaxy's hope for freedom.

Black Jedi clothing

Intercomlink headset

In a quad-laser turret of the *Millennium Falcon*, Luke faces a storm of TIE fighters as the *Falcon* escapes the original Death Star. Despite his inexperience, Luke adapts quickly and destroys two fighters, matching Han Solo's tally and winning the Corellian's respect.

Mechanical hand

Yoda

At first, Luke bridles at Yoda's demanding training techniques

Utility belt

Lightsaber hook

Although he spends only a short time with the wise Jedi Master, Luke learns much from Yoda, who awakens Luke's sleeping abilities and Force sensitivity. The Jedi Master's profound teachings will guide Luke's path of attunement with the Force for the rest of his life.

DATA FILE

◆ Traveling to Dagobah in search of the Jedi Master Yoda, Luke has nothing to go on but his instincts and a vision message from his departed mentor Ben Kenobi.

◆ Returning to his home world of Tatooine, Luke leads the rescue of Han Solo from Jabba the Hutt. Doubted by both his friends and enemies, Luke proves himself and his extraordinary abilities in battle against the Hutt's forces, bringing the fire of Jedi protection and justice back to the galaxy.

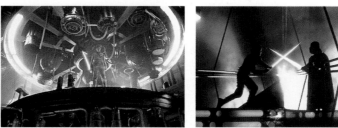

The Shadow of Darth Vader

Growing up, Luke never knew much about his father. Ben Kenobi revealed that Luke's father had been a Jedi Knight, a space pilot, and a warrior, but the secret of his father's death remained clouded by the evil figure of Darth Vader. Only in close combat with Vader does Luke learn the truth that will pose his greatest challenge with the Force.

Princess Leia Organa

STRONG-WILLED and a woman of action, Princess Leia Organa of Alderaan uses her position in the Galactic Senate as a cover for diplomatic aid to the Rebel Alliance. Able to travel throughout the galaxy on her consular ship *Tantive IV*, Leia brings aid to beleaguered planets and secretly makes connections for the Rebellion. A beautiful and pensive young woman, she understands only too well her crucial position at a fateful time for the galaxy, and she hides her personal feelings behind stern discipline and dedication to her cause. As the adoptive daughter of Viceroy Bail Organa, Leia was trained for her royal position by the finest minds on Alderaan. The Princess was highly educated in martial and political arts in a lifelong preparation for her role.

Stolen Imperial blaster

Symbolic belt worn by Alderaan royalty

Traditional gown of the Alderaan royal family

Travel boots

Primary sensor array

Twin turbolasers

Command bridge

Escape pods

Tantive IV

Princess Leia's consular starship is a Corellian Corvette, a common and traditional ship design seen throughout the galaxy. Blending in anonymously amongst galactic space traffic, so many Corvettes have been converted for smuggling or covert uses that they are sometimes called "Blockade Runners."

While on a secret mission to summon the aid of the Jedi Knight Obi-Wan Kenobi, Leia is trapped on board her diplomatic starship. Knowing she will be captured, she nonetheless fights to the end, and does what she can to ensure that her message will reach Obi-Wan, via R2-D2, even if she herself cannot.

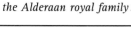

A princess alone within the soulless metal depths of the Death Star, Leia was incarcerated by Darth Vader after her capture. She held firm against every torture.

Princess Leia's influence, royal connections, and diplomatic abilities obtained much of the vital communication and scanning equipment in the Rebel command center on the Fourth Moon of Yavin.

On-duty braids

Rank insignia

Heated vest

White insulated jumpsuit

Boot bindings

Military snow boots

Within the frozen command center of Echo Base, Leia watches the scanners intently for any sign of Imperial detection. Her concerns are always with her people.

When Echo Base is discovered and invaded by Imperial forces, Leia inspires the Rebel pilots, staying at her command post and directing the evacuation even when the base begins to collapse around her.

Although her background has given her little training in mechanical hardware work, Leia does her best to help with repairs when the *Falcon* is in trouble.

Amidst the fabulous beauty of Cloud City, Leia has only a brief time to share with the *Falcon*'s flashy rogue captain before they are all in ensnared in Darth Vader's trap.

Ice Princess

Trading her ceremonial gown for an insulated jumpsuit, Leia still wears symbolic white as the princess of a lost planet in the corridors of Hoth's Echo Base. As the Alliance faces new challenges, she remains a key command figure, directing deployments and determining key strategic moves, with General Rieekan and other Alliance leaders.

Jabba's Slave

Braving the dangers of Jabba's palace in her quest to rescue Han Solo, Leia knew she could face torture or death if captured. Though she did not anticipate the grueling experience of serving as Jabba's slave girl, she endures her captivity with fierce spirit and keeps ready to turn on Jabba when the time is right.

Where dozens of professional assassins had failed, Leia succeeds in putting an end to the contemptible crime lord Jabba the Hutt.

Slave girl harness

Lashaa silk

Jerba leather boots

Rank insignia

Trusty light target pistol

Rebel Leader

Exposed as a Rebel, Princess Leia's career as a recognized diplomat is over, but she contributes more than ever to the strength of the Alliance. No longer content to be just a great symbol, a leader, and a negotiator, Leia also returns to action in the field, proving that she is still one of the best shots in the Alliance.

DATA FILE

◆ Princess Leia is the youngest person ever to hold a seat in the Galactic Senate. Intelligent and a strong leader, Leia is used to taking charge and making things happen.

◆ Trained in military discipline, techniques, and strategy, Leia is an excellent tactician and an expert shot with a blaster. She virtually never misses.

◆ As princess of Alderaan, Leia is a noble leader of her people; as a senator she represents her entire home planet in the Galactic Senate, stirring much sympathy for the Rebellion. Within the Rebel Alliance the princess is a beloved leader and symbol of hope.

Forest Diplomat

Leia's good spirit and natural gift for diplomacy help her to win the confidence of the Ewoks she meets on Endor. By swapping her combat uniform (right) for clothes they make for her, she helps win humble allies that will topple the Empire.

Han Solo

MERCENARY PIRATE, smuggler captain, and cocksure braggart, the overly confident Han Solo is a rugged individual of the Galactic Rim. From impoverished beginnings, Solo worked up through petty thievery to gain a commission in the Academy, from which he was later expelled. A Corellian pilot of the finest caliber nonetheless, Solo gained control of his destiny when he won his ship, the *Millennium Falcon*, in the best game of sabacc he ever played. His reputation as a gunfighter matches his renown as captain of the *Falcon*. Reckless and foolhardy, he is also courageous and daring, a match for any adventure.

Customized blaster pistol

Corellian spacer black vest and light shirt

Faced at gunpoint by one of Jabba's minions in the Mos Eisley Cantina, Han Solo keeps his cool and slowly draws his blaster under the table. The regulars could have warned Greedo that Han was the wrong man to threaten. Only one of them would walk away from the table.

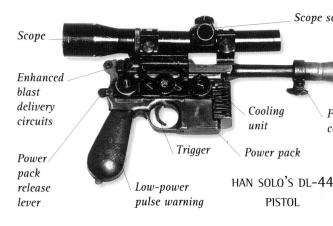

Scope

Scope settings and adjustment

Enhanced blast delivery circuits

Flash suppressor

Power pack release lever

Cooling unit

Final stage collimator

Trigger

Power pack

Low-power pulse warning

HAN SOLO'S DL-44 PISTOL

Droid caller

Blaster power cell

Captain's pants

Corellian blood stripe

Quick-draw holster

Holster thigh grip

Action boots

Captain Solo's loyal friend and first mate is the imposing Wookiee Chewbacca. Each has risked his life for the other in many tight situations. Between Han's fast draw and Chewbacca's violent strength, the two are not to be trifled with.

DATA FILE

◆ As a child Solo was raised by space gypsies, never knowing who his real parents were. He learned tricks and self-reliance from his adoptive community.

◆ Solo's last-minute rescue of Luke Skywalker saved the Rebel Alliance and won him one of the highest medals of honor, along with Chewbacca and Luke Skywalker.

One of Han's regular employers has been the crime lord Jabba the Hutt. When Han had to jettison a cargo to avoid arrest, he incurred Jabba's wrath and was unable to pay him back. This has led to Jabba posting a deadly bounty on Han's head that will haunt him until he resolves the situation.

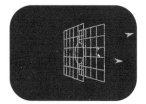

FALCON QUAD-LASER SCOPE

With the *Falcon* on the run and in need of repairs, Han Solo lands at Bespin to meet the ship's previous owner Lando Calrissian, not knowing for certain how Lando will react.

Han in Carbonite

Trapped in a plot by Darth Vader to ensnare his friend Luke Skywalker, Han Solo is taken to the industrial bowels of Cloud City and flash-frozen in carbonite to test the process meant to immobilize Luke. Carbon-freezing is a way of bonding condensed Tibanna gas for transport, but can be used to keep life forms in suspended animation when the painful process of freezing does not kill them.

Millennium Falcon

This battered and aging YT-1300 light freighter has had a long history in the hands of several captains. Han's extensive modifications to the ship have made it one of the fastest vessels in hyperspace. Even at sublight speeds its velocity and maneuverability are extraordinary for a ship of its class. The *Falcon* sports Imperial military-grade armor, quad-laser cannons, a top-of-the-line sensor rectenna, and many other illegal and customized hot-rod components. The ship serves them as a unique home and powerful workhorse.

Han proves to Leia that there is more to being a scoundrel than having a checkered past. A princess and a guy like him?

Han had heard spacer's tales about the legendary titan space slug, but he scoffed at them as nothing more than ghost stories. His narrow escape from the belly of a live space slug restores his distrust in anything being really safe.

Solo, Rebel Leader

After the victory at Yavin, Han eventually accepts a commission as captain in the Rebel Alliance. At frozen Echo Base on Hoth, he volunteers for difficult perimeter patrol duty even though he does not like tauntauns or the cold. Han is a natural leader and serves as an inspiration to many of the troopers around him.

Heavy weather parka

REBEL SENSOR PACK

Extensible antenna

Stentronic wave monitor

Power indicator

Range cycle computer

Power cells

Stolen Imperial electrobinoculars

HOTH EQUIPMENT
With their patrol craft paralyzed by the icy cold, the Rebels must survey the snow plains of Hoth with hand-carried gear. Han Solo is an expert at keeping a low profile and seeing others before they see him, and has helped design the Echo Base perimeter survey plan.

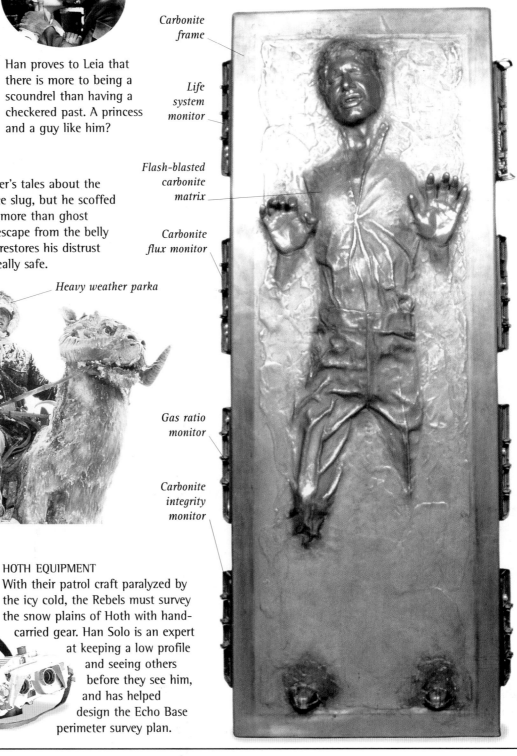

Carbonite frame

Life system monitor

Flash-blasted carbonite matrix

Carbonite flux monitor

Gas ratio monitor

Carbonite integrity monitor

Chewbacca

A MIGHTY WOOKIEE from the planet Kashyyyk, Chewbacca was recued from slavery by the daring Han Solo. Teaming with him to repay the traditional Wookiee life debt, Chewbacca later "adopted" the wayward Corellian and became his best friend. The great Wookiee now uses his mechanical abilities to keep Solo's heavily modified firecracker spaceship flying, and serves as both a fiercely loyal copilot and a trusty fellow adventurer. Chewie enjoys a good fight and likes the action that Solo gets them into, but sometimes acts as his partner's conscience when Han gets a bit too mercenary.

Han Solo and Chewbacca make a dauntless pair of spacers, following adventure where it leads them. The two fight well together, knowing each other's strengths and relying on each other's abilities. Han's ego may get them into trouble or Chewie's temper may start fights, but the two of them together know when to blast 'em and when to run.

Although the *Millennium Falcon* cockpit is small for his great frame, Chewbacca is at ease with the myriad controls and copilots the ship with confidence. Deferring to Han's outstanding marksmanship, Chewie usually flies the ship while Han mans a gun turret during pursuit space combat.

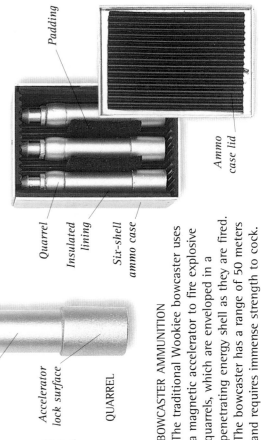

Padding

Quarrel

Insulated lining

Six-shell ammo case

Ammo case lid

Detonator pin

Energy shell flare material

Shell casing

Accelerator lock surface

QUARREL

BOWCASTER AMMUNITION
The traditional Wookiee bowcaster uses a magnetic accelerator to fire explosive quarrels, which are enveloped in a penetrating energy shell as they are fired. The bowcaster has a range of 50 meters and requires immense strength to cock.

Blue eyes

Sensitive nose

Bandolier

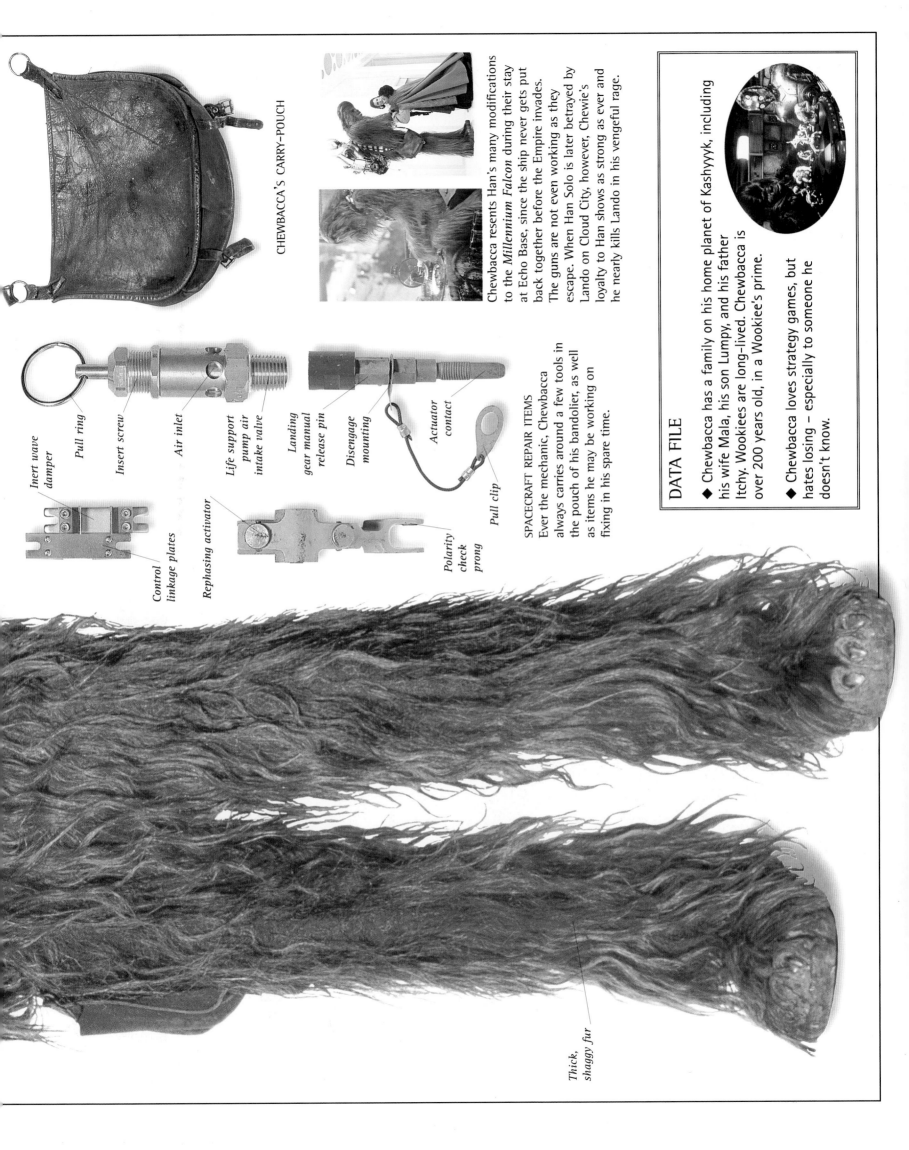

CHEWBACCA'S CARRY-POUCH

Chewbacca resents Han's many modifications to the *Millennium Falcon* during their stay at Echo Base, since the ship never gets put back together before the Empire invades. The guns are not even working as they escape. When Han Solo is later betrayed by Lando on Cloud City, however, Chewie's loyalty to Han shows as strong as ever and he nearly kills Lando in his vengeful rage.

Inert wave damper

Pull ring

Insert screw

Air inlet

Life support pump air intake valve

Landing gear manual release pin

Disengage mounting

Actuator contact

Control linkage plates

Rephasing activator

Polarity check prong

Pull clip

SPACECRAFT REPAIR ITEMS

Ever the mechanic, Chewbacca always carries around a few tools in the pouch of his bandolier, as well as items he may be working on fixing in his spare time.

DATA FILE

◆ Chewbacca has a family on his home planet of Kashyyyk, including his wife Mala, his son Lumpy, and his father Itchy. Wookiees are long-lived. Chewbacca is over 200 years old, in a Wookiee's prime.

◆ Chewbacca loves strategy games, but hates losing – especially to someone he doesn't know.

Thick, shaggy fur

C-3PO
PROTOCOL DROID

In A GALAXY filled with countless cultures and languages, protocol droids assist their masters in matters of etiquette, custom, and translation, assuring that intercultural relations proceed peacefully. C-3PO is fluent in over six million forms of communication and has a strongly programmed desire to see things run smoothly, but neither of these traits prepared him for the turbulent events he would face. Transported into a world of adventure, this pragmatic character is often overwhelmed by the extraordinary action around him, but he faithfully serves his masters.

Keeping an eye out for trouble: 3PO never seems to get through his adventures completely intact. Fortunately, his sturdy components are easily repaired and re-assembled.

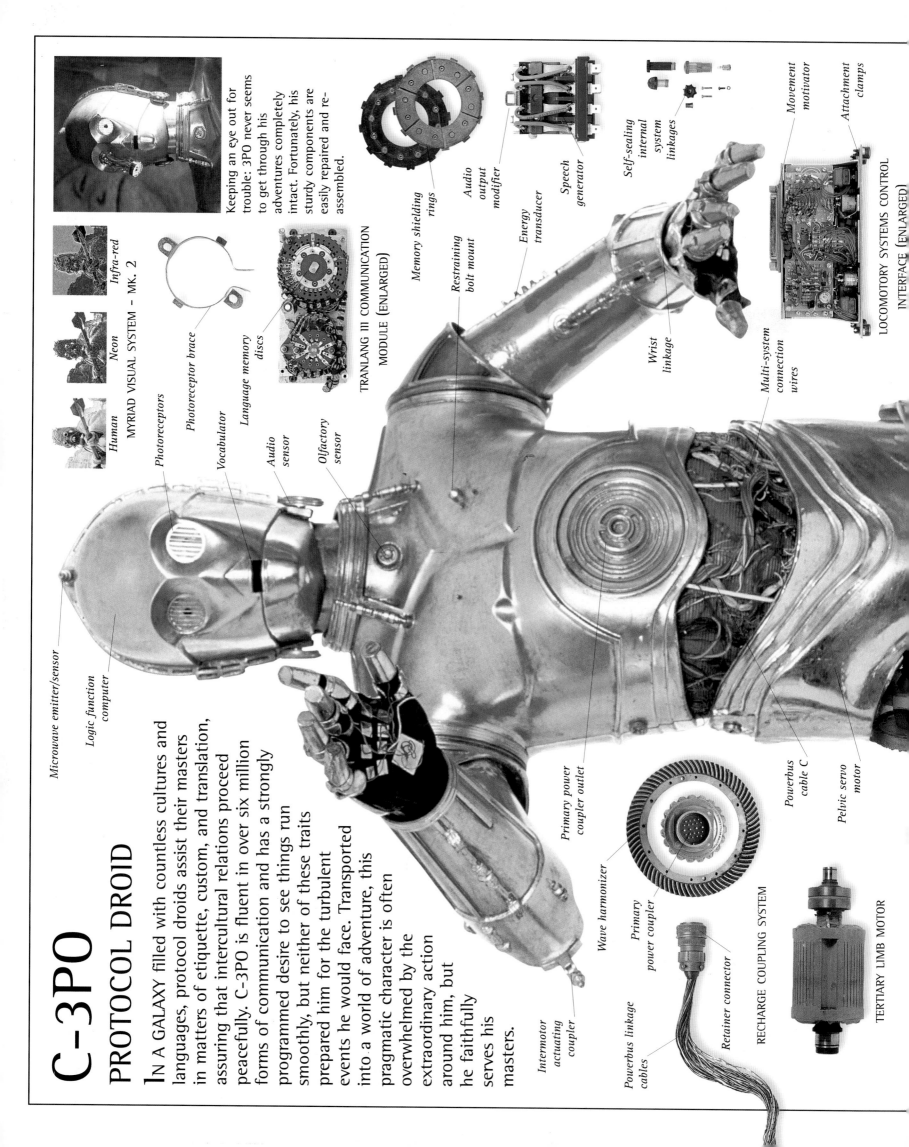

Human   Neon   Infra-red
MYRIAD VISUAL SYSTEM – MK. 2

TRANLANG III COMMUNICATION MODULE (ENLARGED)

LOCOMOTORY SYSTEMS CONTROL INTERFACE (ENLARGED)

RECHARGE COUPLING SYSTEM

TERTIARY LIMB MOTOR

- Microwave emitter/sensor
- Logic function computer
- Photoreceptors
- Photoreceptor brace
- Vocabulator
- Language memory discs
- Audio sensor
- Olfactory sensor
- Memory shielding rings
- Restraining bolt mount
- Energy transducer
- Audio output modifier
- Speech generator
- Self-sealing internal system linkages
- Movement motivator
- Attachment clamps
- Wrist linkage
- Multi-system connection wires
- Primary power coupler outlet
- Powerbus cable C
- Pelvic servo motor
- Wave harmonizer
- Primary power coupler
- Retainer connector
- Intermotor actuating coupler
- Powerbus linkage cables

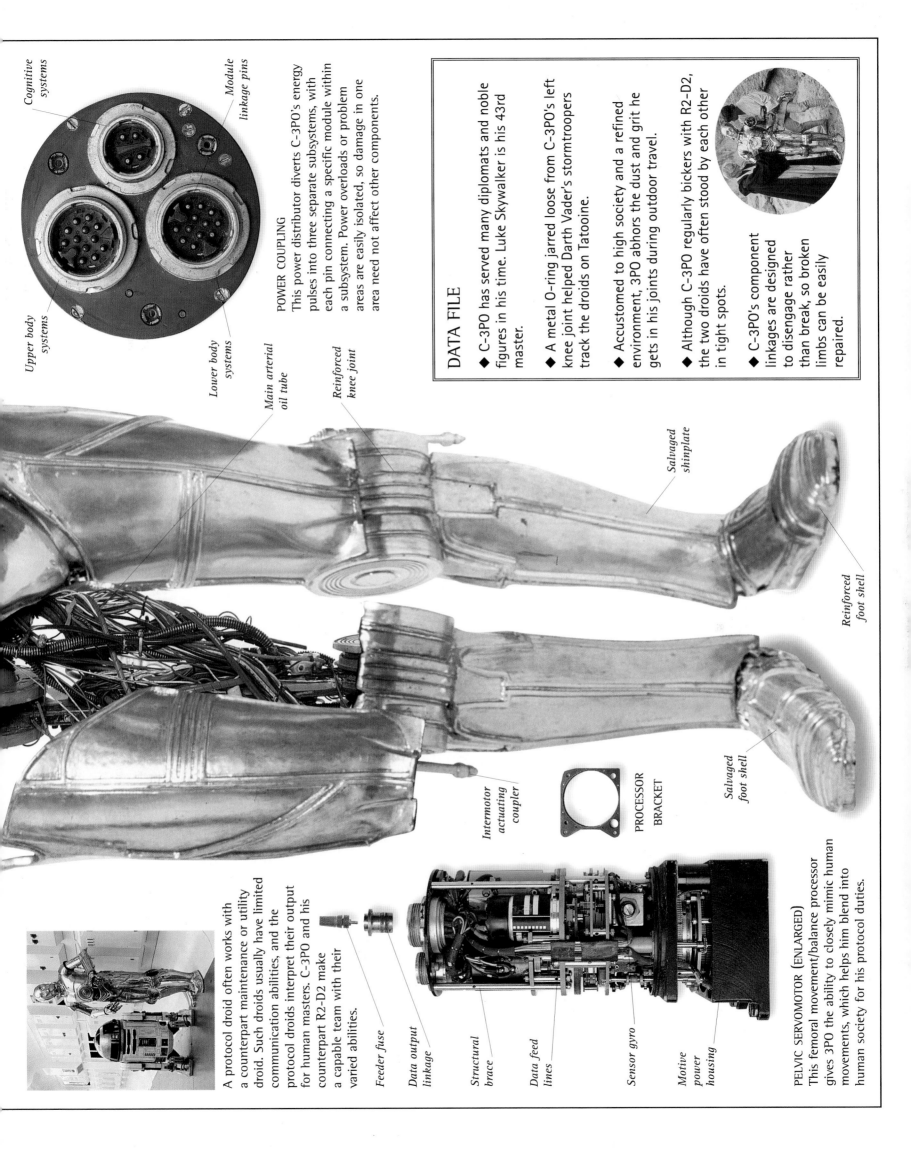

Cognitive systems

Module linkage pins

Upper body systems

Lower body systems

Main arterial oil tube

Reinforced knee joint

POWER COUPLING

This power distributor diverts C-3PO's energy pulses into three separate subsystems, with each pin connecting a specific module within a subsystem. Power overloads or problem areas are easily isolated, so damage in one area need not affect other components.

DATA FILE

◆ C-3PO has served many diplomats and noble figures in his time. Luke Skywalker is his 43rd master.

◆ A metal O-ring jarred loose from C-3PO's left knee joint helped Darth Vader's stormtroopers track the droids on Tatooine.

◆ Accustomed to high society and a refined environment, 3PO abhors the dust and grit he gets in his joints during outdoor travel.

◆ Although C-3PO regularly bickers with R2-D2, the two droids have often stood by each other in tight spots.

◆ C-3PO's component linkages are designed to disengage rather than break, so broken limbs can be easily repaired.

Salvaged shinplate

Reinforced foot shell

Salvaged foot shell

A protocol droid often works with a counterpart maintenance or utility droid. Such droids usually have limited communication abilities, and the protocol droids interpret their output for human masters. C-3PO and his counterpart R2-D2 make a capable team with their varied abilities.

Intermotor actuating coupler

PROCESSOR BRACKET

Feeder fuse

Data output linkage

Structural brace

Data feed lines

Sensor gyro

Motive power housing

PELVIC SERVOMOTOR (ENLARGED)

This femoral movement/balance processor gives 3PO the ability to closely mimic human movements, which helps him blend into human society for his protocol duties.

R2-D2
ASTROMECH DROID

DESIGNED AS a sophisticated computer repair and information retrieval droid, R2-D2 is a highly useful astromech unit filled with apparatus of all sorts. His long history of adventures has given him distinct personality and quirkiness. R2 exhibits a strong motivation to succeed in his assigned tasks, displaying stubborn determination and inventiveness that are extraordinary for a utility droid. A protocol droid like C-3PO must translate his electronic beeps and whistles for human masters, but that doesn't stop R2 from trying to communicate anyway, and he usually manages to get his points across, even without an interpreter. Highly loyal, R2 is never reluctant to risk damage or destruction to help his masters and accomplish missions.

When R2-D2 disappears into a swamp on Dagobah, Luke thinks he may have lost his companion for good ... until R2's periscope pops out of the murky water.

Princess Leia entrusted R2-D2 with the stolen Death Star plans and her urgent message to Obi-Wan Kenobi, which R2 faithfully found a way to deliver. Hologram recording and projection is one of R2-D2's standard capabilities.

An on-board R2 unit is a vital component of the Incom T-65 X-wing. The droid's in-flight adjustments allow for optimum performance. Most pilots would want to use the available droid in the best condition, but Luke Skywalker grows attached to R2-D2 and chooses the droid to accompany him in the attack on the Death Star.

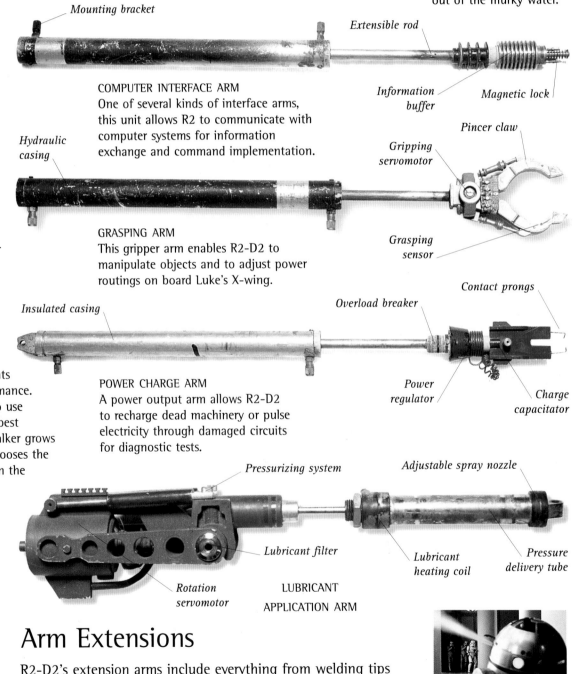

Mounting bracket

Extensible rod

COMPUTER INTERFACE ARM
One of several kinds of interface arms, this unit allows R2 to communicate with computer systems for information exchange and command implementation.

Information buffer

Magnetic lock

Hydraulic casing

Gripping servomotor

Pincer claw

GRASPING ARM
This gripper arm enables R2-D2 to manipulate objects and to adjust power routings on board Luke's X-wing.

Grasping sensor

Insulated casing

Overload breaker

Contact prongs

POWER CHARGE ARM
A power output arm allows R2-D2 to recharge dead machinery or pulse electricity through damaged circuits for diagnostic tests.

Power regulator

Charge capacitator

Pressurizing system

Adjustable spray nozzle

Lubricant filter

Lubricant heating coil

Pressure delivery tube

Rotation servomotor

LUBRICANT APPLICATION ARM

Arm Extensions

R2-D2's extension arms include everything from welding tips to cutter devices, clamps, and magnetic depolarizing leads. Many such devices are built into his various compartments, and an interchangeable component design allows him to be equipped with still others for special tasks.

DATA FILE

◆ Durable and strongly built, R2-D2 has been around even longer than his counterpart C-3PO.

◆ R2-D2 resorts to innovative deceit when necessary, which makes 3PO throw up his hands in dismay. One of R2's deceptions began all of Luke's adventures.

R2-D2 uses his fire extinguisher inventively to conceal his friends from attacking stormtroopers.

Life-scan mesh

Primary photo receptor and radar eye

Logic function display

Data card input

Processor state indicator

Holographic projector

Inert alloy plate

Overload heat vent

MOTIVATOR HOUSING AND VENT

Signal amplifier

HOLOGRAM PROJECTOR BULB

Sensory input head

Head rotation ring

Reinforced rod

Computer interface and lubricant application arms compartment

Spacecraft linkage data slot

Spacecraft linkage and control arms

Hydraulic extension

Actuating coupler

Acoustic signaller

System ventilation

Stored experiences

Main logic processor connection

MEMORY CHIP

SCANNER ANTENNA

Charge arm compartment

MAIN POWER COUPLING

Systems diagnostic input receptors

Interference pulse stabilizers

Grasping arm compartment

Polarity sink

Heat exhaust

Recharge power coupling

Astromech units are standard droid types, and Jabba's personnel found a fitting that would allow R2-D2 to serve drinks on board Jabba's sail barge.

Locomotion power cells

Durasteel shell

Powerbus cables

Third tread (retractable)

Motorized all-terrain treads

21

Lando Calrissian

THE DASHING Baron Administrator of Cloud City has a past that few on Bespin would suspect. As a rogue and con artist, Lando built his early fortunes from modest beginnings, becoming a daring smuggler captain with a good head for business and a bad habit of gambling. He flew the *Millennium Falcon* for years before losing the ship to Han Solo in a sabacc match. The same game later won Lando control of the fabulous gas mining colony on Bespin. As the flamboyant leader of Cloud City, Lando combines his sense of style with a new-found sense of responsibility and has come to enjoy his role as Baron Administrator.

Winning smile

Borrowed Rebel blaster

Tarelle sel-weave shirt

Baron Administrator state belt

Aeien silk lining

Royal emblems

Baron's cape

Handmade Liwari shoes

Cloud City

Suspended high above the core of the gas giant Bespin, Cloud City was once the headquarters of great royal leaders. The city's glorious past has filled the skyline with monumental majesty and ethereal beauty. The city is supported on a single giant column which stems from a processing reactor at its base. In the city's hollow air shaft core are gigantic directional vanes that control the facility's location in space.

Broadcast antenna

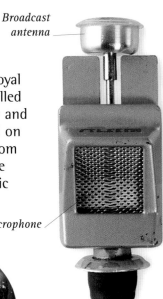

Microphone

Signal processor

COMLINK

Handgrip

Cloud City is home to industrious citizens and advanced technology. Facilities throughout the city process for export the rare anti-gravitational tibanna gas from the exotic atmosphere of Bespin.

Calrissian is forced to betray Han Solo and his friends to Darth Vader in order to preserve Cloud City's freedom. When Lando learns that Vader has no intention of keeping the bargain, he plots a rescue and escape with his aide Lobot.

General Lando

Having become a renegade on the run from the Empire, Lando fell in with the Rebels after leaving Cloud City. His penetrating judgment at the Battle of Tanaab won Lando promotion within the ranks, and the former con artist and baron became a general within the Alliance. He once more wears a cape of honor and authority. Grown beyond his self-centered past, Lando still finds adventure but now contributes his abilities to a greater cause.

Electro-stun extensible bayonet

Stun attachment wire

Vibro blade

Vibration generator

Blade release switch

Rank insignia

Dress cape

Rank plaque

Alliance general's uniform

Sidearm blaster

Wrist comlink

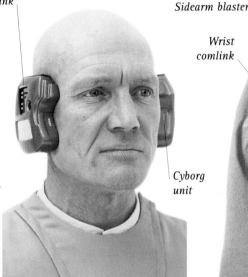

City central computer link

Cyborg unit

Lobot

Equipped with cybernetic implants, the Chief Administrative Aide of Cloud City keeps in direct contact with the city's central computer. Able to monitor a vast array of details at once, Lobot is an ideal assistant to Lando Calrissian. Lobot takes great satisfaction in making Cloud City a well-run success.

By turning against the Imperial forces of Darth Vader, Lando loses everything he has built as Baron Administrator of Cloud City. Racing through the corridors of the city with Leia and Chewbacca, Lando witnesses Boba Fett lift off with Han Solo, and barely escapes with his life from the city he once ruled.

Grip

Blade/electro-stun power unit

Reinforced lance pole

VIBRO-AXE
POLEARM

Disguised as a lowly skiff guard at Jabba's palace, Lando braves the very heart of danger to rescue Han Solo. His old con man skills are put to good use, and no one at the palace ever suspects him until it is too late.

DATA FILE

◆ Using a comlink and his security code, Lando can address all parts of Cloud City from any central computer terminal.

◆ Lando uses an old underworld contact on Tatooine to secure a guard job at Jabba's palace.

Obi-Wan Kenobi

JEDI KNIGHT

FAR OUT in the remote Jundland wastes lives the hermit Ben Kenobi. Ben is a figure of mystery to the Tatooine settlers, dismissed by many as a crazy wizard. In truth Kenobi is a Jedi Knight, a great warrior of the Old Republic who fought in the Clone Wars. One of Kenobi's students turned to the dark side of the Force, betraying the Jedi and assisting the rise of the Emperor. Crushed by his failure with the man who became Darth Vader, Kenobi retreated to Tatooine, watching over the young Luke Skywalker and waiting for the time to reveal Luke's birthright as the son of a Jedi. Kenobi's powers make him a threat to the Empire even in his elder years.

Hooded cloak

Jedi robes

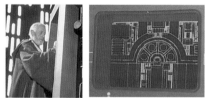

In accordance with Jedi philosophy, Kenobi lives simply. In his hut are only a few scant reminders of his former life and great exploits. It is here that Kenobi gives Luke his father's lightsaber.

Hovering training remotes are used by Jedi and also by gunfighters to sharpen reflexes and develop coordination. They can be set to varying degrees of aggressiveness and their shock rays adjusted from harmless to painful.

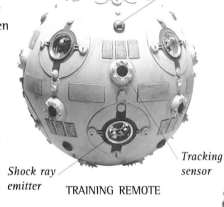

Air jet

Shock ray emitter

TRAINING REMOTE

Tracking sensor

On board the Death Star, Kenobi uses his technical knowledge and Jedi mind powers to disable a crucial tractor beam without being noticed. This is his first return to such heroic action in many years.

Even after he is struck down by Vader, Kenobi returns in spirit to guide Luke on his path to becoming a Jedi. On Hoth and near death, Luke sees Kenobi just before being rescued by Han Solo.

It is Kenobi who first awakens Jedi abilities in Luke and begins to train him, but Luke can learn from him only briefly before Kenobi faces his final lightsaber duel. Afterward, as Luke learns the ways of the Force, he is able to meet Ben again in spirit.

DATA FILE

◆ Ben Kenobi once rescued Luke when the boy had become lost in the Tatooine wilderness with his friend Windy. In spite of this, Owen Lars forbade Kenobi from ever coming near their farm again.

◆ Luke Skywalker returns to the home of Ben Kenobi to build his own lightsaber after losing his father's in the battle on Cloud City.

Yoda
JEDI MASTER

NOT TO BE JUDGED by his small size, the wise Jedi Master Yoda is very powerful with the Force. At almost 900, his years of contemplation and training have given him deep insight and profound abilities. One of his greatest challenges is the training of Luke Skywalker, who arrives on Dagobah an impatient would-be Jedi. In the short time he has with Luke, Yoda must instill in him the faith, peace, and harmony with the Force that will fulfill Luke's potential and guard him from the dark path of temptation, anger, and evil. To his final student Yoda imparts the heart of the ancient Jedi traditions that are the galaxy's last hope.

Jedi robes

Through the Force, Luke Skywalker is able to see his mentors Yoda and Obi-Wan, as well as his father Anakin, all finally at peace due to Luke's heroic efforts. United in the Force, their Jedi spirits are restored and complete.

On Dagobah, Yoda uses his attunement with the natural world to live peacefully on the resources around him. His gimer stick, for example, serves as a walking staff as well as a source of pleasant gimer juice, which can be chewed out of the bark.

HEALING EARTH-ROCK

Dagobah

A remote planet of swamps and mists, inhospitable Dagobah hides a tremendous variety of life forms, including gnarl trees, butcherbugs, and swamp slugs. This inhospitable setting provides a good hiding place in the dark days of the Empire.

YARUM SEED
tea-making variety

MUSHROOM SPORES

GALLA SEEDS

SOHLI BARK

Green skin

Sensitive ears

Gimer stick

Tridactyl feet

Yoda spends his days in meditation, seeing ever deeper into the infinite tapestry that is the living vitality of the Force. Like Obi-Wan, he hides behind an assumed identity of harmless craziness. Yoda uses this persona to test Luke upon his arrival on Dagobah. As Obi-Wan once told Luke, "Your eyes can deceive you. Don't trust them."

DATA FILE

◆ Yoda's house expresses his oneness with nature, using no technological appliances or fittings. All the furnishings in the house of clay, sticks, and stones were handcrafted by Yoda himself.

◆ In the days before the sinister Empire, Yoda held a seat within the Jedi high council on the Republic's capital world of Coruscant.

Rebel Leaders

HARD-PRESSED for ships and weapons, the Rebel Alliance relies on its capable leaders to make the most of every asset. Living up to the highest standards of virtue and duty, they come from many backgrounds – from nobility and powerful government positions to mechanics, pilots, and merchants who have answered the call of justice and freedom. A good Rebel leader can overcome the Empire's numeric advantage with inventive tactics, or find the words and deeds needed to bring new allies into the fight for freedom. The Alliance recognizes merit, and capable individuals soon find themselves in positions of authority.

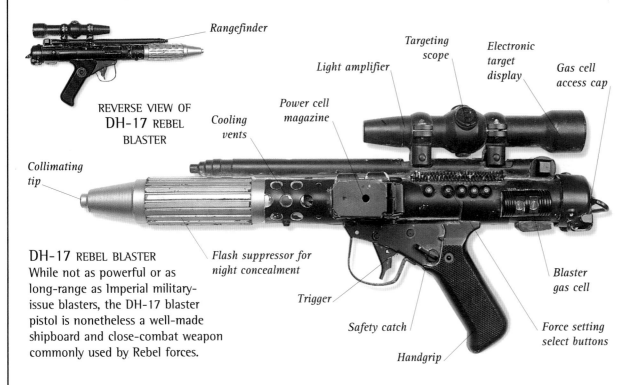

Rangefinder

REVERSE VIEW OF DH-17 REBEL BLASTER

Targeting scope

Light amplifier

Electronic target display

Gas cell access cap

Cooling vents

Power cell magazine

Collimating tip

DH-17 REBEL BLASTER
While not as powerful or as long-range as Imperial military-issue blasters, the DH-17 blaster pistol is nonetheless a well-made shipboard and close-combat weapon commonly used by Rebel forces.

Flash suppressor for night concealment

Trigger

Safety catch

Handgrip

Blaster gas cell

Force setting select buttons

Carlist Rieekan

The grim General Rieekan keeps the seven hidden levels of Echo Base in a state of constant alert, ever wary of discovery by Imperial forces. The terrible cold of Hoth made patrolling the perimeters of the base difficult until Rebel craft could be adapted to the ice.

The frozen world of Hoth is home to Echo Base, where the Rebels retreat after the discovery of their base on the Fourth Moon of Yavin. Hoth provides protection only for a short time before an Imperial probe droid detects the Rebel presence.

Jan Dodonna

General Jan Dodonna is a dauntless master tactician, commanding the Rebel assault on the Death Star in the Battle of Yavin. While the stolen plans provided a complete technical readout of the Death Star, the station seemed invulnerable. General Dodonna identified the one best hope of penetrating the station's defenses and bombing a small thermal exhaust port. His strategy enabled a small fleet of 30 one-man fighters to annihilate a battle station over 160 kilometers wide.

The Rebel forces won their first victories against the Empire from hangars hidden deep within ancient temples in the remote, jungled Fourth Moon of Yavin.

The tactical display at the Massassi base on Yavin 4 tracks the Death Star as it orbits Yavin, closing in to destroy the Rebel stronghold. The display offers limited ability to zoom in and monitor the movements of the ships in battle.

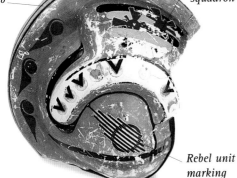

Reinforced midrib

Pre-Rebellion squadron insignia

Rebel unit marking

REBEL HELMET
Battle leaders are as vital to the Rebellion as strategic masterminds. The battered helmet of X-wing squadron Red Leader Garven Dreis testifies to his extensive battle service.

Admiral Ackbar

Commander of the Rebel fleet, the cautious Admiral Ackbar hails from the ocean world of Mon Calamari. Once a slave to Grand Moff Tarkin, Ackbar was rescued by Rebels and convinced his people to join the Alliance. The giant Mon Cal star cruisers contributed by his people are the largest ships in the Rebel fleet.

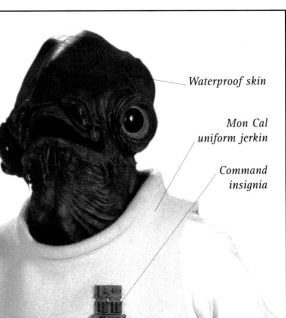

Waterproof skin

Mon Cal uniform jerkin

Command insignia

Admiral Ackbar commands the Rebel fleet from his seat in his personal flagship, the Headquarters Frigate, a Mon Calamari star cruiser contributed to the Alliance by his people.

Chandrillian Freedom Medal

Their secret bases discovered or destroyed, the Rebels fled into space to escape the Empire. The Alliance maintains a mobile command center on board the Mon Cal Headquarters Frigate, from where the actions of the fleet are directed.

Mon Mothma

Mon Mothma is the highest leader of the Rebellion. As a member of the galactic Senate, Mon Mothma championed the cause of freedom until the Emperor's evil closed in around her. Abandoning the Senate, she built the Rebel Alliance and continues to strengthen it through her diplomacy and negotiations.

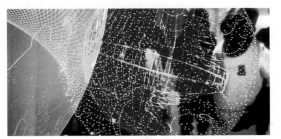

A tactical monitor in the Alliance command center displays the defensive shield projected around the second Death Star from the Forest Moon of Endor. This display also reveals interior areas of the Death Star.

DATA FILE

◆ The Rebellion is greatly aided by the Bothan spynet, a galaxy-wide secret organization of daring operatives who claim to be able to obtain nearly any information, for a price. Bothan teams will endure heavy losses to accomplish their objectives.

◆ This 300-meter-long Nebulon B escort craft serves as medical frigate for the Rebel fleet.

Utility belt

Moisture-retaining fabric

Positive grip shoes

Tauntauns

THE SNOW LIZARDS called tauntauns are one of the few forms of life that thrive in the frozen conditions of the ice planet Hoth. Several different breeds of tauntaun live in various terrains on Hoth, from herds moving across moss-covered tundra to the solitary mountain tauntauns and small packs of lichen-eaters dwelling deep within the ice caves. Tauntauns survive the intensely cold nights by slowing their metabolisms almost to a standstill, and can die if forced into activity once the night cold descends.

TAUNTAUN HEAD

TAUNTAUN SKULL

Tauntaun Patrols

Tauntauns serve the Rebel troops of Hoth's Echo Base more reliably than patrol vehicles, which are often halted by the winds and cold. Snow-dwelling tauntauns were domesticated and trained early on during the construction of Echo Base. Tauntauns make obedient and hardy mounts, but they secrete thick oils and have an unpleasant odor. Patrol riders learn to ignore this, and ride their tauntauns on constant lookout for Imperial forces.

Horns for dominance combat

Ears

Cap warmer

Reins

Rebel patrol scout

Saddle

Survival gear

Thick oily fur

Oil glands

Tough lips for scraping lichen

Internal organs protected within layers of fat and muscle

Hoth

Hoth is uninhabitable except for a subarctic band circling its equator. The Rebels' Echo Base is located on the snowy northern edge of this band. Most tauntauns live in the equatorial tundra and subsist on lichen and ice worms.

Tail for balance when running

Strong leg muscles

Stirrups

Claws for clearing ice from lichen

Tridactyl feet

DATA FILE

◆ Tauntauns are irritated by the ultrasonic frequencies of certain droids, such as this tactical 3PO unit, and tend to swat them with their tails. The droids of Echo Base have learned to be careful.

◆ Many of the Rebels' tauntaun patrol mounts were discovered living in the ice caves that became Echo Base.

On several occasions, tauntauns were killed in the stables of Echo Base by wampa ice creatures stalking the caverns and corridors at night. The medical droids analyzed the wounds and determined their origin.

Medical Droids

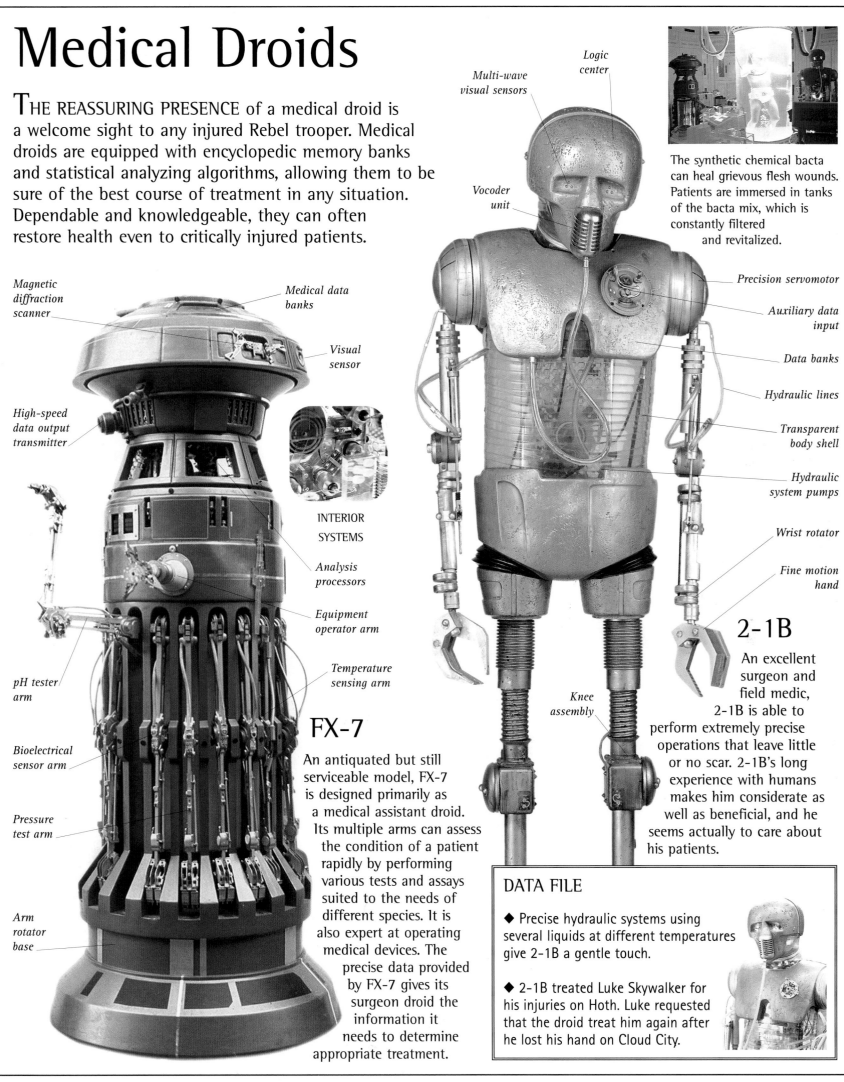

THE REASSURING PRESENCE of a medical droid is a welcome sight to any injured Rebel trooper. Medical droids are equipped with encyclopedic memory banks and statistical analyzing algorithms, allowing them to be sure of the best course of treatment in any situation. Dependable and knowledgeable, they can often restore health even to critically injured patients.

Multi-wave visual sensors

Logic center

Vocoder unit

The synthetic chemical bacta can heal grievous flesh wounds. Patients are immersed in tanks of the bacta mix, which is constantly filtered and revitalized.

Magnetic diffraction scanner

Medical data banks

Visual sensor

High-speed data output transmitter

INTERIOR SYSTEMS

Analysis processors

Equipment operator arm

pH tester arm

Temperature sensing arm

Bioelectrical sensor arm

Pressure test arm

Arm rotator base

Precision servomotor

Auxiliary data input

Data banks

Hydraulic lines

Transparent body shell

Hydraulic system pumps

Wrist rotator

Fine motion hand

Knee assembly

FX-7

An antiquated but still serviceable model, FX-7 is designed primarily as a medical assistant droid. Its multiple arms can assess the condition of a patient rapidly by performing various tests and assays suited to the needs of different species. It is also expert at operating medical devices. The precise data provided by FX-7 gives its surgeon droid the information it needs to determine appropriate treatment.

2-1B

An excellent surgeon and field medic, 2-1B is able to perform extremely precise operations that leave little or no scar. 2-1B's long experience with humans makes him considerate as well as beneficial, and he seems actually to care about his patients.

DATA FILE

◆ Precise hydraulic systems using several liquids at different temperatures give 2-1B a gentle touch.

◆ 2-1B treated Luke Skywalker for his injuries on Hoth. Luke requested that the droid treat him again after he lost his hand on Cloud City.

Darth Vader

A GRIM, FORBIDDING FIGURE, Darth Vader stalks the corridors of the Imperial Navy. Once regarded as mad human wreckage, with the increasing favor of the Emperor Vader has risen in power and influence to become a much-feared military commander. Grand Moff Tarkin was one of the few who recognized Vader's capabilities in spite of his bizarre appearance and eccentric conduct, and as Tarkin's right-hand man Vader attained a new level of respect amongst the upper echelons of the Imperial military. Unable to survive without the constant life support provided by his suit, Vader is nonetheless a powerful figure whose knowledge of the dark side of the Force makes him unnerving and dangerous.

Vader rose through the Imperial ranks fighting the resentment and contempt of higher officers. Along the way, Vader earned the respect and fear of line troops and commanders for his bold actions and front-line command presence.

Magnetic sensor pits

Speech projector and respiratory intake

Respiratory vent

Neck vertebra replaced with metal

Outer cloak

Vision enhancement receptors

Armored breast plate to shield badly injured chest

Cybernetic replacement internal organs

Control chestplate

Control function connectors

Artificial cyborg lower arm

Vader allows no one to assist him with his accoutrements. In a special isolation chamber, mechanical arms assist in the removal and replacement of certain of his suit components.

CHESTPLATE
Vader's life support systems are monitored and controlled through this central panel of chestplate controls on his suit. Slots allow the insertion of diagnostic cards for periodic system checkouts, while switch panels allow function modification.

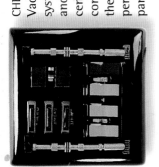

System function indicator

Control activator; only when this is pushed will Vader's chestplate controls work

Secondary system function box

Electromagnetic clasp

DARTH VADER'S BELT

Synthetic belt strap

Primary system function box

Vader plotted with the Emperor to sway Luke to the dark side. In an intense lightsaber battle, Vader tempted Luke with the proposal that the two of them join to overthrow the Emperor. Where Vader's loyalties really stood at this time is lost in the darkness filling his soul.

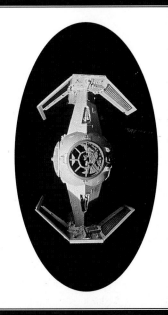

Body heat regulators

Outer helmet locking surface

Multiple power cells

Hermetic seal

Power distributor

Helmet air pump

Electrical system radiators

Hermetic seal

Neck support

Voice processor

Nutrient feed tube

Armored boots binding cyborg elements to flesh

Primary environmental sensor

Air processing filter

INTERIOR OF VADER'S HELMET
Vader's helmet is the most important part of his life support suit, connecting with a flat backpack to cycle air in and out of Vader's broken lungs and keeping his hideously damaged skull in shape.

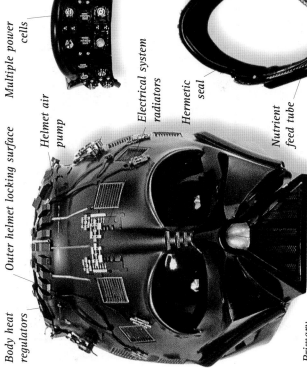

Anakin Skywalker

The horror and tragedy of Darth Vader are revealed when he tells Luke Skywalker "I am your father." Vader hopes to bring Luke down the same dark path of hate and anger that destroyed Anakin Skywalker. Instead he finds that Luke is committed to finding redemption for his father in spite of all that Vader has become.

TRACKING MONITOR
This Death Star tracking monitor shows the Fourth Moon of Yavin emerging from behind the planet itself into firing range.

Imperial Leaders

THE EMPEROR'S WILL is enforced by the might of the Imperial Space Navy and its assault forces. Imperial military commanders carry out the orders of the Emperor and hold the true positions of power in the New Order. The price for failure can be death, but ambition for the highest posts keeps competition fierce amongst officers. While bureaucracy and political whims can place incapable men in high posts, many of the Empire's commanders are formidable military talents in a system that values ruthless efficiency.

Superlaser

Exhaust port

THE FIRST DEATH STAR
The Death Star contains a hypermatter reactor that can generate enough power to destroy an entire planet. Invulnerable to large-scale assault, the space station has a fatal weakness in a small thermal exhaust port (connecting directly to the main reactor) which can be bombed by a small fighter craft.

Docking bays

Aboard the original Death Star, this conference room can project holographic tactical readouts for evaluation by Tarkin and his Imperial strategists.

Grand Moff Tarkin

Governor of the Imperial Outland Regions, Grand Moff Wilhuff Tarkin conceives the horrific Death Star superweapon as part of his doctrine of Rule by Fear. The Imperial Outlands contain systems too scattered to police effectively, but the fear of the Death Star will subjugate systems across the galaxy.

SUPERLASER TARGETING DISPLAY

DEATH STAR GUNNERS
Obeying the orders of their superiors, gunnery crew leaders ensure that the titanic energies of the Death Star laser systems do not overload or hit phase imbalances that would cause huge internal explosions.

Imperial Navy emblem

Antenna

Officer tunic

Imperial officer's disc

Rank insignia plaque

Imperial code cylinder

Officer's disc

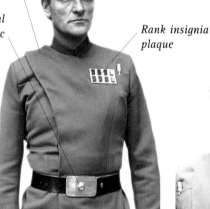

ADMIRAL PIETT

ADMIRAL OZZEL

Transceiver

Shielded lens

DEATH STAR GUNNER'S HELMET

Neutral-alloy helmet

General Veers

General Maximillian Veers masterminds the devastating Imperial assault on Echo Base, commanding the action in person within the lead walker cockpit. A cunning and capable individual, Veers is a model Imperial officer.

Tunic

CAPTAIN NEEDA

MOFF JERJERROD

Emperor Palpatine

IN THE LAST DAYS of the Republic, Senator Palpatine used deception to become elected President of the Galactic Senate. Once in office he appointed himself Emperor. He declared martial law throughout the galaxy and began to rule through the military forces of the newly-created Imperial Navy. Palpatine affected the simple clothing of a simple man, but drew his powers of persuasion and control from the blackest depths of the dark side of the Force. While the Force has twisted his face, it has also sustained him beyond his years, and even in his old age the Emperor remains a figure of terrible power.

Hood to hide face

Simple cloak

Superlaser weapon

Unfinished structure

Axial power column

The Emperor's ceremonial arrivals are attended by thousands of massed stormtroopers and air parades of fighter wings.

THE SECOND DEATH STAR
The Emperor conceived the second Death Star as a colossal trap, which would use a false image of vulnerability to lure the Rebel fleet into fatal combat.

Coruscant headwear

IMPERIAL
SHUTTLE

On board the second Death Star, the Emperor's throne room surveys the stars from atop a high isolation tower.

Imperial Dignitaries

The Emperor's favor can elevate individuals to positions of fantastic galactic power. High officials owe their posts to Palpatine's whim, and form a society of twisted sycophants and back-stabbers.

Emperor uses cane because he pretends to be weak, not because he needs it

DATA FILE

◆ Mysterious and fanatically loyal Imperial Royal Guards protect the Emperor wherever he travels.

◆ Imperial Royal Guards are so highly trained in deadly arts that their chosen weapon is not a blaster but a vibro-active force pike, which they use with lightning swiftness to inflict precise and lethal wounds.

Imperial Stormtroopers

IMPERIAL STORMTROOPERS are first-strike units sent into critical combat situations in support of both the Imperial Star Fleet and the Imperial Army. Highly disciplined and completely loyal to the Emperor, stormtroopers carry out their orders without hesitation and without regard to their own lives. These grimly anonymous troopers turn the might of their training and weaponry on any opposition to the Empire with utterly ruthless efficiency. Shielded in white space armor worn over a body glove, stormtroopers are protected from harsh environments, projectile and impact weapons, and glancing blaster bolts. Equipped with the finest and most powerful arms and equipment, they are the most trusted and most effective troops in the Imperial military, and the most deeply feared opponents of the Rebel fighters.

While Imperial Army or Navy forces may be assigned to keep order, stormtroopers are sent in to crush initial resistance and do the toughest fighting. Stormtrooper boarding parties are systematic and professional in taking charge of a captured ship.

Body glove

Plastoid composite armor

Thermal detonator

Utility belt

Energy sinks absorb blast energy

Blaster holster

Suit systems power cells

Short-range combat pistol

Manual suit seal and environmental controls

Blaster power cell container

Reinforced alloy plate ridge

Sniper position knee protector plate

Combat de-ionizer

Positive-grip boots

UTILITY BELT TOOLS
Standard-issue equipment in the utility belt includes power packs, energy rations, and a compact tool kit. The belt can carry additional gear such as a grappling hook, comlink, macrobinoculars, handcuff binders, or other items such as this combat de-ionizer.

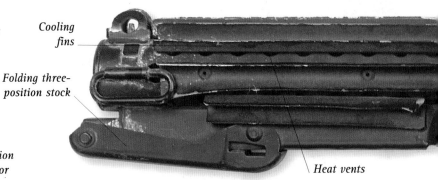

Cooling fins

Folding three-position stock

Heat vents

Stormtrooper Blaster

The E-11 BlasTech Standard Imperial Sidearm combines excellent range with lethal firepower in a compact and rugged design. A standard power cell carries enough energy for 100 shots. Replacement cells are carried in a trooper utility belt. Plasma gas cartridges last for over 500 shots and the unit features an advanced cooling system for superior fire-delivery performance. A folding three-position stock converts the weapon to a rifle configuration for sustained long-distance firing.

Often deployed and paraded in overwhelming numbers, the stormtrooper legions are adept at manipulating the psychology of dominance, shielded in the eerie anonymity of their armor.

CODE
TRANSMITTER

Series code

Pocket clip

Data interface

Officer's disc

STORMTROOPER OFFICER'S CAP

BELT BUCKLE

OFFICER'S RANK PLAQUES

CODE CYLINDERS

Reinforced helmet

Broadband communications antenna

Audio pickup

Stormtrooper Officers

In non-combat situations, stormtrooper officers wear distinctive black tunics and caps. Their insignia – officer's discs, rank plaques, and code cylinders – conform to the standards of the Imperial Navy. Code cylinders allow officers access to secure areas and computer systems. All stormtrooper officers are proven soldiers, and in combat they wear body armor like any other trooper. Officers in field units may wear colored shoulder pauldrons as high-visibility rank indicators.

Power cell

Range-finding sight

Accessory mounting rail

Setting adjust

Gas cartridge cap

Energy ration

Blast energy sink

Safety catch

Low-power pulse indicator

Magnatomic adhesion grip

In battle, stormtroopers are disciplined to ignore casualties within their own ranks. Notice is only taken from a tactical standpoint. They are never distracted by emotional responses.

DATA FILE

◆ A power pack and pressurized gas system in the stormtrooper armor backplate allows a trooper to survive even in the vacuum of space for limited periods. For extended exposure to open space, troopers wear space backpacks with extended life-support capacity.

◆ Stormtrooper armor is impervious to projectile weapons and blast shrapnel. It may be pierced by a direct blaster bolt, but will deflect glancing bolts and reduce damage from bolts absorbed.

STORMTROOPER ARMOR
Every component of a stormtrooper's armor and equipment is manufactured to the highest standards in the Empire. Their armor lasts indefinitely and may still be found half-buried at decades-old battle sites.

Stormtrooper Equipment

WHILE THE BRUTAL TRAINING and intense conditioning of stormtroopers accounts for much of their power and effectiveness, Imperial-issue stormtrooper equipment is also vital in making them the galaxy's most dreaded soldiers. Field troops carry gear such as pouches of extra ammunition (power packs and blaster gas cartridges) and comprehensive survival kits. Standard backpack sets can adapt troopers to extreme climates or even the vacuum of space. Component construction allows standard backpack frames to be filled with gear suited to specific missions, which may include micro-vaporator water-gathering canteens, augmented cooling modules, or a wide variety of base camp and field operative equipment.

Under able officers like Commander Praji, stormtrooper teams adapt to their environments. The unpredictable sandstorms of Tatooine can immobilize landing craft, but native dewback lizards carry search parties equipped with desert gear through any conditions.

With high-powered backpack communications gear, troopers in Mos Eisley alerted orbiting Star Destroyers to intercept the escaping *Millennium Falcon*.

Acoustic sensors

Folding tines

Fibercord reel

GRAPPLING HOOK

Comlink

The hand-held comlink supplements a stormtrooper's built-in helmet transmitter/receiver system with improved range and communication security. Comlink sets can be tuned with sophisticated encryption algorithms to work only with each other. Within or near Imperial bases, comlink signals are boosted and relayed automatically for optimal transmission.

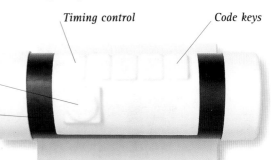

Timing control   *Code keys*

Detach control

Axidite shell

Thermal Detonator

Stormtroopers are usually issued a thermal detonator, carried at the back of the belt. Controls to set arming, timing, and blast intensity are not labelled so that enemy troops cannot use the powerful explosives if they are captured. While these detonators would not normally be used against intruders on board an Imperial ship or battle station, troopers carry their full set of standard equipment at all times to maintain combat readiness and familiarity with the feel of their gear.

Rangefinder

Electronic sight

BLASTECH DLT-20A LASER RIFLE

Firing capacitor   *Cooling vents*   *Galven circuitry barrel*

Power charge system

Magnatomic adhesion grip

Laser Rifle

In field combat situations, the standard Imperial sidearm offers insufficient accuracy at long range. Field troops are issued blaster rifles, which improve the consistency and accuracy of blaster bolt trajectory by incorporating additional collimating rings and longer conduits of galven circuitry. Imperial blaster rifles are extremely rugged weapons, which give Imperial troops a deadly edge in battle. They are much prized on the black market.

DATA FILE

◆ Stormtrooper backpack gear can include boosted field communication sets, mortar launchers, and equipment for establishing security perimeters.

◆ Squad leaders, who lead units of seven troopers, wear orange shoulder pauldrons.

Activator

POWER CELLS
Small power packs plug into standard stormtrooper gear,
including standard helmets and back plates as well as
communication sets and other field equipment. Complex
circuitry extracts the maximum power from the cell.

Stormtrooper Helmet

There are a number of different models of Imperial
stormtrooper standard issue helmets, incorporating
various specialized components and changing over time
with new developments. In this model, enhanced
optical equipment creates holographic images of the
surrounding terrain, shielding the eye from excessive
brightness and offering vision through many barriers
such as smoke, darkness, and fire. Optical equipment
in trooper helmets can range from simple eye
lenses to these elaborate vision processors.
The helmets are cooled and atmosphere-
processed to keep the trooper operating
at peak efficiency
at all times.

4 layer
construction

Outer plastoid
composite armor

Inner
insulator

Anti-laser mesh

Magnetic shielding layer

Comtech Series IV
speaker uses
three-phase sonic
filtering for
clear sound

Atmospheric
cycling
unit

Padding

Power cell

Atmosphere
intake and
processing unit

Used air exhaust

Artificial air
intake

Voice filtering unit

Comlink
microphone

Mouth plate

Artificial air supply nozzles

Specialist Stormtroopers

FOR ANY MILITARY SITUATION there is an appropriate class of Imperial soldier, well-equipped for environments that would challenge the standard stormtrooper. Certain Imperial troopers are selected at an early stage for specialization and conditioned with appropriate knowledge and psychological training. Once specialized, their psychological conditioning to their particular identity is so strong that a trooper almost never wishes to change his division.

Helmet

Polarized snow goggles

Breath warmer cover

Chest plate

Imperial sidearm

Heated pants

Rugged ice boots

Wrist comlink

Insulating belt cape

Legs less heavily armored, for mobility

The E-Web heavy repeating blaster can be broken down into its component parts and carried into difficult snow terrain or through restricted ice passages by a crew of only a few troopers. With weaponry such as this, specialized troopers can destroy any advantage the Rebels hope to gain from unusual terrain.

Adjustable attachment straps

Communications unit

Accessory power outlet

Heater

Surplus power indicator

Heater liquid pump

Blast armor

Reinforced blast plate

Power indicator

Homing beacon

External temperature monitor

Communication controls

Identity chip

Suit heater controls

Power cell monitor

Rations storage compartment

Heavy-duty power cell

SNOWTROOPER CHEST PLATE

SNOWTROOPER BACKPACK

Snowtrooper

Equipped with breath heaters under their face masks, snowtroopers are self-sufficient mobile combat elements. Their backpacks and suit systems keep them warm and exceptionally mobile for environments of ice and snow. They can survive for two weeks in deeply frozen environments on suit battery power alone.

The ground troops of General Veers' Blizzard Force on Hoth find themselves accompanied at the Echo Base invasion by the extraordinary figure of Darth Vader. Vader oversees the occupation of the base with the front line of the assault group.

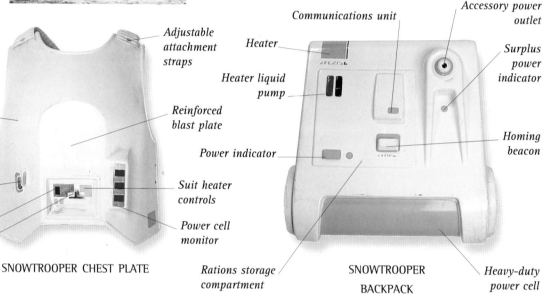

Terrain sensor

Guidance vanes mounting strut

Forward guidance repulsor field directional vanes

Speeder bike

The light repulsorlift Imperial speeder bike carries one or two riders at high velocities for reconnaissance and antipersonnel missions. An unusual turbine repulsorlift makes the bike stable even in extreme maneuvers. Forward-reaching repulsor fields help thread it through obstacles like trees, but their guidance must be used carefully because they are not strong enough to deflect the bike away from obstacles on their own.

Scout Trooper

Scout troopers are equipped for high maneuverability and long periods without support. Trained to an unusual degree of independence for Imperial personnel, scout troopers are nonetheless conditioned to work with partners wherever possible. Scout troopers are armored only on the head and upper body. They carry food supplies, micro-cords, and other gear that allows them to reach and silently infiltrate almost any objective, far from resupply by Imperial forces.

In the dense forests of Endor, biker scouts patrol the perimeters of the Imperial shield generator and its garrison, wary and watchful for troublesome forest creatures or terrorist infiltrators. Working in units of two or four, they coordinate their efforts for superior surveillance coverage.

Electro-magnetic vision enhancement visor

Boosted comlink system for long-range communication

Body glove

Power unit backpack also stores gear

Survival rations

Survival kit

Acceleration handgrip

Repulsor guide settings

Power management setting

Steering lever

Tracking sensor

Steering sensitivity adjust

Repulsor drive

Braking linkage

Guidance linkage

Brake pedal

Turbine repulsorlift

DATA FILE

◆ Other specialized Imperial trooper divisions include flying airtroopers, liquid-borne seatroopers, tunneling underminers, and Magma troopers who crush revolts on volcanic mining worlds.

◆ Scout troopers have motion sensors and enhanced macrobinocular viewplates allowing them to see energy emissions, night vision, and designated target magnification.

Phase amplifier

Targeting scope

Short-range laser emitter

Mini gas cell

Grip retainer guard

SCOUT TROOPER BLASTER

Imperial pilots

IMPERIAL FIGHTER PILOTS are an elite group within the Imperial naval forces. Only ten percent of those accepted into training graduate with commissions. Through their intense psychological conditioning, pilots are entirely dedicated to target destruction and know that their mission comes above all other concerns, including those of personal survival and aid to threatened wingmen. Each pilot knows he is expendable. TIE pilots are trained to regard the TIE craft as the most expressive instrument of Imperial military will, and they exult in their role, taking pride in their total dependence on higher authority.

Reinforced flight helmet

Ship-linked communi- cations

Gas transfer hose

Life support pack

Vacuum g-suit

Energy-shielded fabric

Positive gravity pressure boots

Air scrubber

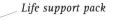

TARGETING READOUTS
TIE targeting systems are superior to anything available to Rebel fighters. The advanced readouts of these Seinar systems track targets in high resolution.

Emitter aperture

JAMMING UNIT

TIE FIGHTER FUELING PORT
TIE fighter fuel is a radioactive gas under high pressure. The twin ion engines of the ship have no moving parts, making the TIE easy to maintain.

Solar array

Fueling port

TIE Fighter

The standard TIE fighter carries no deflector shield or hyperdrive equipment and employs high-performance ion engines energized by solar array "wings." This lightweight design makes the craft lethally agile, but leaves the pilot defenseless and unable to travel far from his base station. TIE pilots view shields as tools of cowards.

DATA FILE

◆ Pilots rely on their self-contained flight suits to stay alive in space, as TIE fighters contain no life support systems.

◆ TIE fighters have no landing gear and are launched from special hangar racks.

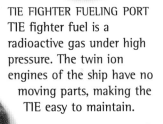

Reinforced helmet

Imperial Army emblem

Pressure hose

Life support pack

Air hose

AT-AT Pilots

Drawn from hardened combat soldiers, All Terrain Armored Transport (AT-AT) pilots are conditioned to believe themselves invincible. Though they no longer need their armor and life-support suits, they continue to wear them – perhaps as part of their combat history. AT-AT pilot training makes these men masters at guiding the mighty walkers through irregular terrain or city streets, wreaking destruction and terror.

AT-ST Walker Pilots

The All Terrain Scout Transport (AT-ST) is able to move in and through terrain too dense or irregular for full-size Imperial AT-AT walkers. Their pilots are chosen for superior sense of balance and dexterity with the walker controls, since scout walkers must be able to move quickly through the unexpected to accomplish their missions of reconnaissance and anti-personnel hunting.

Suit heat control

Energy monitor

System linkage

Receptor filaments

Echo transmitter

Signal amplifier

Identity chip

AT-AT TARGETING SENSOR

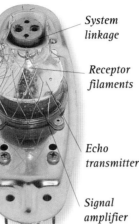

Forests and rugged inclines are easily managed by the small, gyroscopically-stabilized AT-ST, or scout walker. Its range is limited since it is too small to carry a full-size locomotion power generator and fuel.

POWER PACK CONTROL UNIT

Comlink

Slide mount rails

Energy monitor contact

Driving gauntlet

SURVIVAL SYSTEM POWER PACK
The advanced design of the Imperial field life support pack worn by AT-AT pilots allows a single power cell to run suit systems and heating for up to five days without requiring recharge. The power cell is self-managing and extracts maximum output from its matrices.

Command and navigation center

Assault troops staging area

Gear harness

Insulated jumpsuit

Insulated boot

DATA FILE

◆ AT-ATs are not climate-controlled, so pilots venturing into frozen terrain must wear special insulated suits.

◆ AT-AT pilots are recruited from the strongest combat troops.

AT-AT Walker

These gigantic machines are used as terror weapons. Their powerful walking controls can only be operated by pilots of great physical strength. Until the Battle of Hoth, AT-ATs were widely regarded as invincible in combat, and their mere appearance was often enough to drive enemy forces into fearful retreat.

Imperial Droids

THE EMPIRE'S MILITARY FORCES adapt common droid models to suit specific Imperial purposes and also commission specialized new forms, including illegal assassin and torture droids. Imperial droids are programmed with extremely harsh identity parameters, restricting their abilities for independent action and focusing them tightly on their assigned tasks. This can make them oblivious to external circumstances. Imperial droids are pure machines which rarely develop anything approximating personality.

When Princess Leia refused to discuss the location of the hidden Rebel base, Darth Vader brought in a torture droid. Leia had heard rumors of such atrocities, but hoped they were not true. Subjected to the machine's horrible manipulations, Leia somehow maintained her resistance even near the point of death from the pain.

Mouse Droid

While often used to carry messages, MSE (or "mouse") droids are also used in vast Imperial ships and battle stations to lead troops through long mazes of corridors to their assigned posts. Since they each include complete readouts of their assigned sections, they are programmed to melt their processors instantly upon capture. This gives them an odd combination of paranoia and self-importance.

Electroshock assembly

Life energy monitors

Sonic torture device

Chemical torture turret

Sonic piercing needle

Searing flesh pincers

Acid jet

Durite housing

Biofeedback monitors

Drug injector

Hypnotic power strip

Victim analysis photoreceptor

Lower repulsor projector

Magnetic fault sensor

Circuit fault detector

Logic housing

Function commence indicator

Audio receptor

Motorized leg

Victim pain response monitors

Arc emitter

R4-19

When patrolling the corridors of the Death Star, computer maintenance and repair units go about their tasks automatically, servicing only the equipment and areas permitted to them. Their perception limited for security reasons, they are oblivious to all but their programmed work.

Interrogator Droid

Illegal by the laws of the Republic, this interrogation droid is one of the technological horrors concocted behind the curtains of Imperial secrecy. Completely without pity, this nightmare machine surgically exploits every physical and mental point of weakness with flesh peelers, joint cripplers, bone fragmenters, electroshock nerve probes, and other unspeakable devices. It injects drugs to heighten excruciating pain and erase mental resistance while forcing victims to remain conscious.

Probe Droid (Probot)

Carried to their destination planets in hyperdrive pods, intelligent and eerie probe droids relentlessly search the galaxy for evidence of Rebel presence. Floating above the ground on repulsorlifts and drifting mysteriously on silenced thrusters, probots are equipped with myriad sensors and investigative instincts. They are programmed to find out a location's secrets, communicating their discoveries to distant Star Destroyers via high-frequency HoloNet transceivers.

The Imperial Mark IV patrol droid IM4-099 moves through the streets of Mos Eisley on the lookout for criminal activity or illegal signal emissions. It is equipped with no weapons, but sounds an alarm and transmits an alert on detection.

DATA FILE

◆ Many Imperial utility droids are equipped with secret spy devices that allow human overseers to monitor military personnel, ensuring obedience.

PROBOT SENSOR PLATE

A probot sent out from the Star Destroyer *Avenger* detects the Rebel base on Hoth and sends its images of the power generators back to Darth Vader.

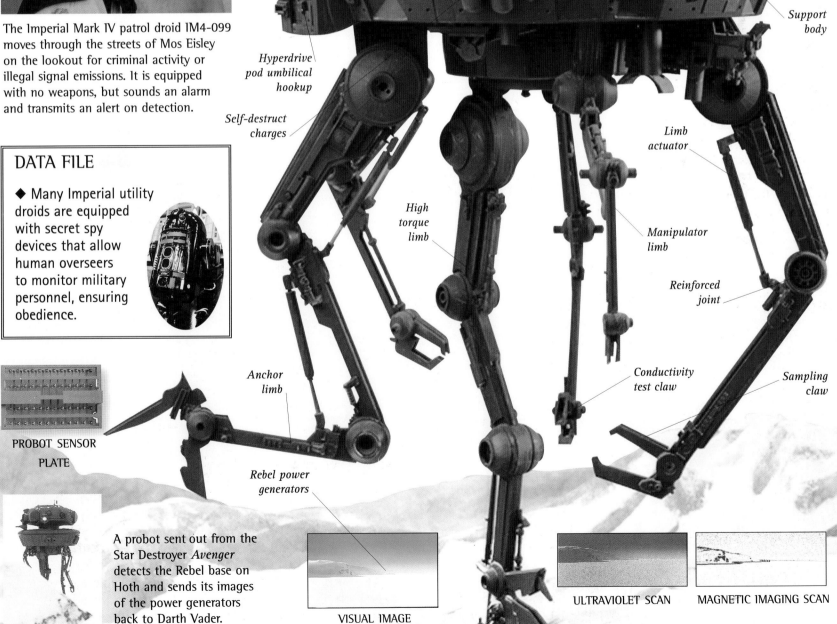

Radiation meter

High-frequency transmission antenna

Sensor head

Transmitter dome

Light armor

Holocam

Magnetic imager

Motion sensor

360-degree high-sensitivity sonic sensor

Defense blaster

Support body

Hyperdrive pod umbilical hookup

Self-destruct charges

Limb actuator

High torque limb

Manipulator limb

Reinforced joint

Anchor limb

Conductivity test claw

Sampling claw

Rebel power generators

VISUAL IMAGE

ULTRAVIOLET SCAN

MAGNETIC IMAGING SCAN

43

Jabba the Hutt

Jabba's palace is equipped with many security devices, including a semi-intelligent droid gatewatcher built into several of the entrances.

AT THE CENTER of an extensive crime empire is the repellent crime lord Jabba the Hutt. Equipped with a cunning criminal mind, Jabba has built his syndicate through a long history of deals, threats, extortion, murders, and astute business arrangements. Unlike many of his competitors, Jabba is highly intelligent, and rarely overlooks details or dangers. Once bold and daring, he has settled back in his old age to a life of debauchery in his palace on Tatooine. Jabba enjoys violent entertainment almost as much as he enjoys profits, and he arranges deadly gladiatorial games and creative executions on a regular basis.

JABBA'S TATTOO, OF YORO ROOT PIGMENT

Telepath response unit

Brain support unit

Locomotion unit

Neurix tube

Spider leg

Detachable brain jar

Disembodied monk brain

Manipulator claw

B'OMARR MONK
Automated droid legs carry disembodied monks through the palace. The oldest spider droids have four legs, while more recent models have six.

Alkhara's Tower

Main citadel

Western Keep

The desert palace of Jabba the Hutt was originally a monastery constructed long ago by the mysterious B'omarr monks. Over the years, bandits took control of parts of the citadel, adding portions even as the monks went about their secret ways in the nether reaches of the structure. As Jabba's headquarters, the fortress holds a wide variety of gangsters, assassins, travelers, crooked officials, entertainers, and servants.

Oola

Oola was kidnapped from a primitive clan by Jabba's majordomo Bib Fortuna, and trained by other Twi'lek girls in the art of seductive dance. Although Jabba finds her highly desirable, Oola refuses to give in to him.

Lekku (head-tail)

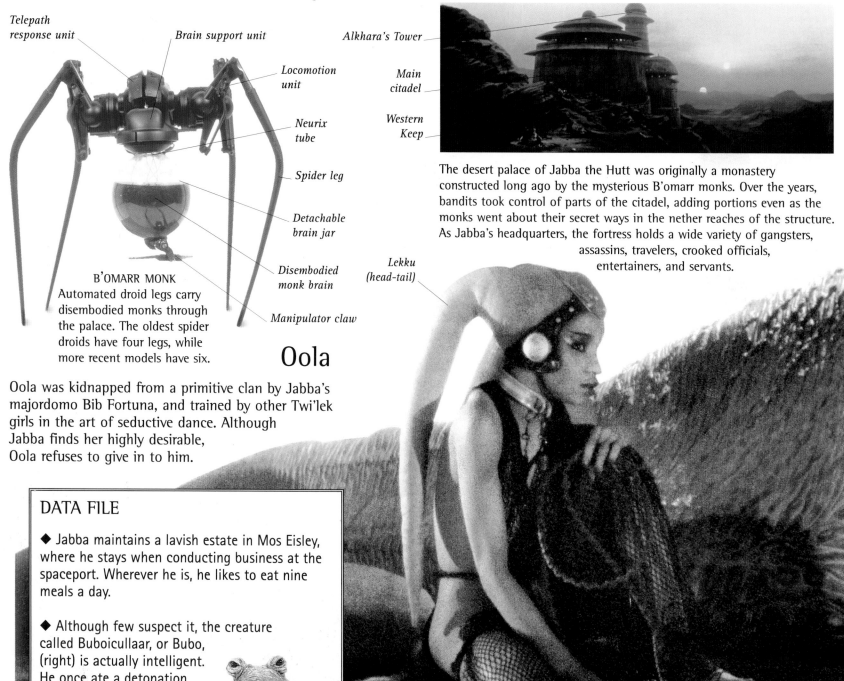

DATA FILE

◆ Jabba maintains a lavish estate in Mos Eisley, where he stays when conducting business at the spaceport. Wherever he is, he likes to eat nine meals a day.

◆ Although few suspect it, the creature called Buboicullaar, or Bubo, (right) is actually intelligent. He once ate a detonation link needed for a bomb, foiling an attempt to assassinate Jabba.

Jabba the Hutt

Jabba Desilijic Tiure, known to all as simply Jabba the Hutt, comes from the planet Nal Hutta, where he was raised (by his father, also a crime lord) to crave power and wealth. Hutts are notorious for their ruthless and amoral ways, and they often exploit their physical power to control weaker species. Hutts run most of the galaxy's large criminal syndicates.

Muscular body can move like a snail or slither forward

Accompanied by lookouts on sand skiffs, Jabba's sail barge *Khetanna* carries the Hutt on journeys to Mos Eisley or to places of execution and gladiatorial combat staged for the crime lord's amusement.

Internal mantles shape a Hutt's head

Hutt skin secretes oil and mucus, making Hutts difficult to seize

Body has no skeleton

Hermi Odle

Ephant Mon

Hookah pipe

Naal thorn burner

Jabba's palace is filled with bizarre creatures like his personal armorer, the Baragwin Hermi Odle. The former gunrunner Ephant Mon is Jabba's only real friend: the Hutt once saved his life.

Salacious Crumb

When Jabba first found this Kowakian monkey-lizard stealing his food, he tried to eat him, but later he became amused by the creature's antics. Salacious has since taken on the job of Jabba's court jester.

Salacious Crumb

Movable dais

Jabba's Entourage

CROWDED AROUND JABBA is a wide variety of individuals — sycophants, co-conspirators, hired thugs, and beings of mystery. The crime lord's extensive syndicate offers opportunity to many types, just as Jabba's power and wealth draw many to secretly scheme against him. The Hutt regards the inevitable plots as amusement, pitting the different schemers against each other before compassing their destruction. Amidst all the power plays and convoluted ambitions, many are individuals simply doing their jobs and ignoring the web of intrigue around them. Each in the retinue have their own stories, and curious paths have led every one of them to the desert palace.

Sensory brain areas

Scary red eyes

Sharp, pointed teeth

Lekku (head-tail; one of two)

Dagger (concealed in robe)

Slaver bracelet

Traditional Ryloth robe made from Jalavash worm silk

Soft-soled shoes for silent movement

Rock wart sting juice (dried)

Chall granules

Krayt dragon venom

Taulek style handle

TWI'LEK DAGGER AND POISONS

Poisoned blade

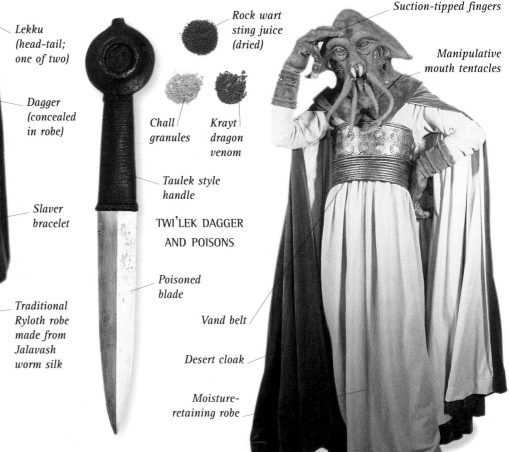

Suction-tipped fingers

Manipulative mouth tentacles

Vand belt

Desert cloak

Moisture-retaining robe

Bib Fortuna

Jabba's Twi'lek majordomo supervises the affairs of both the desert palace and the Mos Eisley estate. Before working with Jabba the Hutt, Bib Fortuna grew wealthy as a slave trader of his own people and became a hunted criminal as a spice smuggler. As Jabba's chief lieutenant, he plots to kill his boss behind a facade of obsequious manners. Fortuna's control within the organization and his tendency to resort to underhanded means with friends and foes alike make him a powerful and dreaded, if cowardly, individual.

A clever Qarren from Mon Calamari, Tessek views the world of Jabba's palace with a clear and calculating mind. As Jabba's accountant, he embezzles money into a secret fund and plans (like several others) to assassinate Jabba and take over his organization.

Jabba finds Bib Fortuna serviceable but not up to the standards of his best majordomo, Sevan Domna, who was killed in an assassination attempt on Jabba decades ago.

Barrel

Simple optical targeting scope

Heat sink

Phase amplifier

Trigger

Recharge valve

SKIFF GUARD'S BLASTER

Nostrils

Thick oily pelt

Hooked claw

Calloused skin

Most Eloms are sympathetic to the Rebellion, but this vile opportunist carries out extortion activity for Jabba, interacting with few others at the palace.

Jabba's skiff guards serve as escorts and lookouts, fully exposed on the skiffs to wind, sun, and enemy fire. New hires generally get skiff duty.

Retractable eyes

Tusks

Coarse fur

J'Quille is a brutal Whiphid from the cold planet of Toola, working as a manhunter for Jabba. He is actually a spy for a rival crime lord, and is planning to kill the Hutt with a slow-acting poison in his food.

Gamorrean Guards

Tough, brutish Gamorrean guards stand throughout Jabba's palace as sentries. Prone to violence, these slow-witted creatures are stubborn and loyal. The low intelligence of male Gamorreans is an asset to their employers, as they cannot be bribed or persuaded to betray. They prefer hand-to-hand combat weapons over blasters.

Helmet

Sensitive nose

Thick muscles

Shoulder armor

Gauntlets

Vibro-lance

Weak eyes

Palace garments

Fangs

Heavy-duty ax head

Sandals

Jabba's Entertainers

Yarna d'al Gargan has been a dancer at the palace for years. She is the daughter of an Askaji tribal chief, brought by slavers to Tatooine, then bought by Jabba. While she still resents the Hutt, she is close to some palace regulars.

JABBA HAS COME TO SPEND a good deal of time in his palace, importing entertainers to amuse him in his courts. His wealth and lavish spending can attract real talent, but the palace reputation for danger and mayhem tends to keep out all but the desperate. The bands that do end up playing the palace are typically either slaves to debt, heavy spice users, or the singing dregs of galactic society. Some few are merely very poor judges of venue, and those that leave the palace intact almost always fire or eat their managers. Jabba's whims keep this odd flotsam of musicians and dancers hopping, one way or another.

These singers were appalled to find out what life at Jabba's palace is really like. They put on a show of enthusiasm with each performance, desperately trying to figure out how to get out alive.

Ak-rev

Umpass-stay

Power drum

Jabba's drum master Ak-rev grew up in a Sriluurian monastery devoted to Am-Shak, the god of thunder, where he learned to play the thunder drums of the temple. Ak-rev is assisted by the Klatoonian Umpass-stay, who is secretly also a bodyguard for Jabba.

The Rodian Doda Bodonawieedo has become the favorite bard of Jabba's palace Gamorreans. At times he plays with the palace bands. Barquin D'an is the brother of Bith Figrin D'an of the Modal Nodes.

Barquin D'an with kloo horn

Traz

Lekku (head-tail)

Form-fitting szona body glove

Hooves

RYSTÁLL

Suction-tipped fingers

GREEATA

Sounding cymbal

Resonator

Radion modulator

Plandl horn

Xloff horn

Troomic sound tube

Sub-woofer base

BONTORMIAN KLESPLONG

When he particularly likes a unique sound, Jabba keeps the instruments of some bands that ... don't need them anymore. These exotic instruments stay in the palace, and the Hutt sometimes orders the new bands to perform using them, even if they don't know how.

Sensua bindings

Dance shoes

The body shape of Hutts makes them unsuited to elaborate forms of dance, but Jabba has developed an appreciation for the sinuous and rhythmic movements of non-Hutt dancers. A good dancer can obtain the favor and indulgence of the Hutt, and those who are also expert at the arts of manipulation can find profit or opportunity among his entourage.

Lyn Me

A Twi'lek from the barren northern continent of Ryloth, Lyn Me practiced the arts of seductive dance to make her way off-planet. Max Rebo talked her into coming to Jabba's palace.

DATA FILE

◆ Quite a few more bands have arrived at the palace than have left. When really disappointed, Jabba feels entitled to feed bad musicians to his rancor.

◆ Known on his homeworld as Rapotwanalantonee, Max Rebo's Shawda Ubb plays a combination flute and water organ.

Droopy McCool

Totally oblivious to what's going on around him, this Kitonak hardly recognizes the stage name given to him by Max Rebo. A far-out quasi-mystic, he hardly fits in with the Rebo band but doesn't notice; he just plays his tunes. Lonely for the company of his own kind, he claims to have heard the faint tones of other Kitonaks somewhere out in the Tatooine dunes.

Sy Snootles

Misled by Jabba's enthusiastic appreciation, the egotistical singer Sy Snootles has a very inaccurate view of her own potential. As a vocalist she is too weird to make it anywhere mainstream. She will probably never discover this, since Jabba's favorite singers find it very hard to leave the palace.

Max Rebo

The blue Ortoloan known in the business as Max Rebo is a half-insane keyboard player completely obsessed with food. He accepted a contract with Jabba that pays only in free meals, to the outrage of his bandmates. He may have poor judgement as a band leader, but he is devoted to music and quite good at his chosen instrument.

Keen sense of smell

Ears store fat

Output speaker

Air intake

Fingertips can absorb food and drink

RED BALL
JET ORGAN

Keyboard

Organ base

Air outlet pipes

Boba Fett

A MYSTERIOUS BOUNTY HUNTER with his own code of honor, Boba Fett wears a customized suit of Mandalorian battle armor from another era – battered, scarred, and still lethally effective. Disguised behind his helmet, his origins are enigmatic. Fett takes only certain assignments, but devotes himself to those few with fanatical skill. His cool and calculating ways together with his manifold hidden capabilities have brought in many "impossible" marks, and earned his reputation as the best bounty hunter in the galaxy. From the concealed weapons covering his space suit to the disguised armaments of his starship *Slave I*, Boba Fett is unerringly a bounty's worst nightmare.

Boba Fett has worked for Darth Vader on several occasions, enough to have been called Vader's right-hand man. Vader finds Fett an intelligent, ruthless, capable ally, worthy to track Rebels and pursue Luke Skywalker.

Slave 1

Rotating cockpit capsule

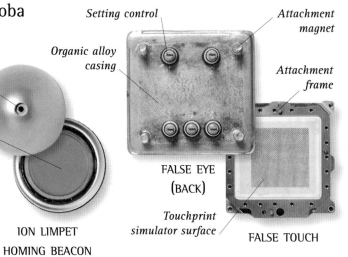

Boba Fett's distinctive starship is an aging, heavily-modified police craft jammed with weapons and customized tracking equipment of every kind, as well as a stolen military sensor masking system to hide him from those he stalks. Four on-board power generators are required to run the many weapons systems that can suddenly deploy from hidden panels.

Setting control

Organic alloy casing

Attachment magnet

Attachment frame

ION LIMPET
HOMING BEACON

HoloNet transmitter

S-thread detection matrix

FALSE EYE
(BACK)

Touchprint simulator surface

FALSE TOUCH

Boba Fett uses these devices to track his marks and gain silent access to high security areas. A false touch pad clamps over touchprint locks to simulate the bioelectrical field and fingerprint of nearly any individual. A false eye pad can be applied to defeat retinal scan locks in a similar fashion. The ion limpet quietly uses the galactic HoloNet to track spacecraft throughout the known galaxy.

Jet Backpack

Missile

Fett's backpack is an excellent combination jumper-pack and rocket launcher. The launcher can be fitted with a missile or with a grappling hook projectile (attached to a rope and winch). The jet jumper system holds rocket blasts for short flights or for escaping and surprising Boba's prey.

Missile boost charge

Stabilizing gyro

Jet Pack adjustment tool

Fuel tank

Directional servo

Missile launcher

Missile targeting rangefinder

Activation button

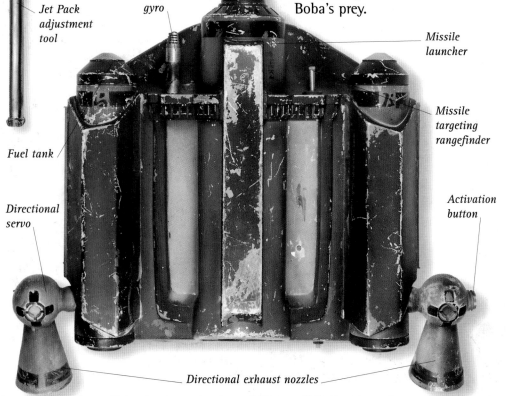

Directional exhaust nozzles

DATA FILE

◆ Fett is notorious for completely disintegrating those whom he has been hired to track down and kill.

◆ Working as a spy for Darth Vader, Boba Fett first encountered Luke Skywalker on a moon in the Panna system, where he almost tricked Luke into giving away the new location of the main Rebel base.

◆ Fett's services are famously expensive, but his honor cannot be bought. He only accepts missions which meet his harsh sense of justice.

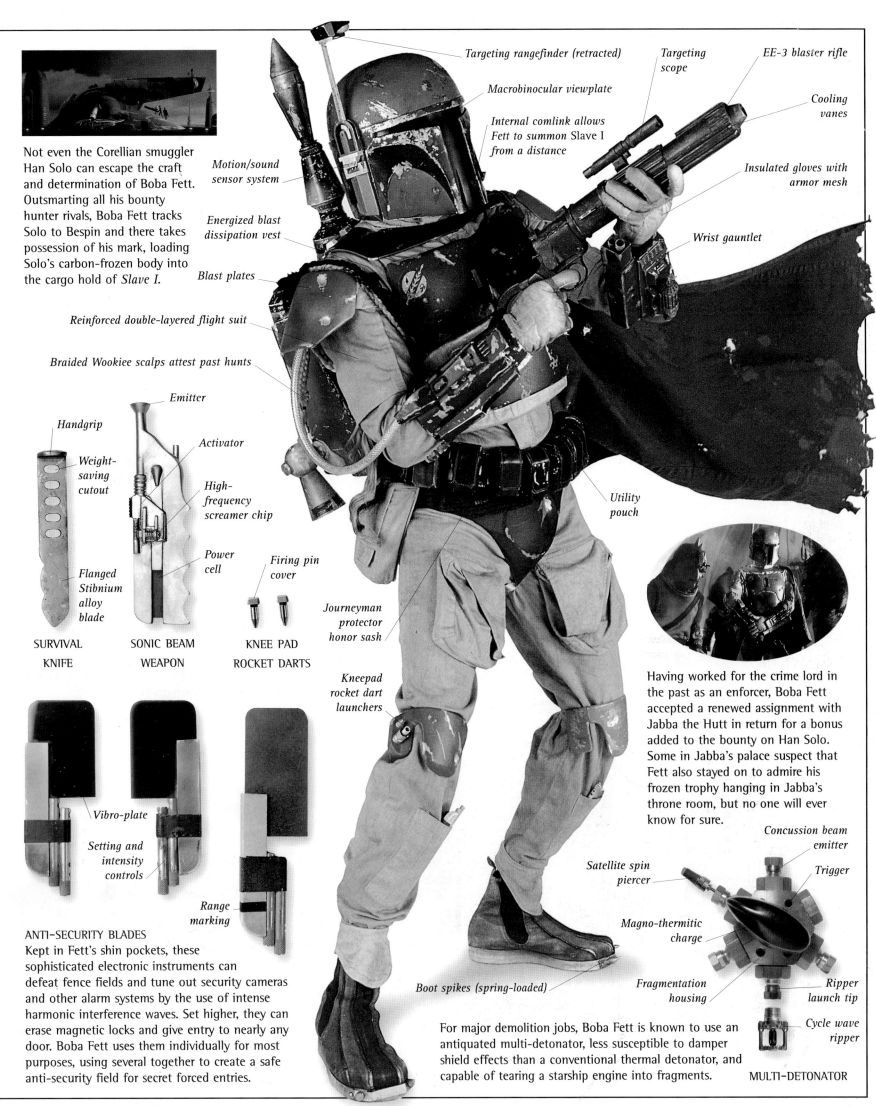

Not even the Corellian smuggler Han Solo can escape the craft and determination of Boba Fett. Outsmarting all his bounty hunter rivals, Boba Fett tracks Solo to Bespin and there takes possession of his mark, loading Solo's carbon-frozen body into the cargo hold of *Slave I*.

Targeting rangefinder (retracted)

Targeting scope

EE-3 blaster rifle

Macrobinocular viewplate

Internal comlink allows Fett to summon Slave I from a distance

Cooling vanes

Motion/sound sensor system

Insulated gloves with armor mesh

Energized blast dissipation vest

Wrist gauntlet

Blast plates

Reinforced double-layered flight suit

Braided Wookiee scalps attest past hunts

Handgrip
Emitter

Weight-saving cutout

Activator

High-frequency screamer chip

Power cell

Firing pin cover

Flanged Stibnium alloy blade

Utility pouch

Journeyman protector honor sash

SURVIVAL KNIFE

SONIC BEAM WEAPON

KNEE PAD ROCKET DARTS

Kneepad rocket dart launchers

Having worked for the crime lord in the past as an enforcer, Boba Fett accepted a renewed assignment with Jabba the Hutt in return for a bonus added to the bounty on Han Solo. Some in Jabba's palace suspect that Fett also stayed on to admire his frozen trophy hanging in Jabba's throne room, but no one will ever know for sure.

Vibro-plate

Setting and intensity controls

Range marking

Concussion beam emitter

Satellite spin piercer

Trigger

Magno-thermitic charge

ANTI-SECURITY BLADES
Kept in Fett's shin pockets, these sophisticated electronic instruments can defeat fence fields and tune out security cameras and other alarm systems by the use of intense harmonic interference waves. Set higher, they can erase magnetic locks and give entry to nearly any door. Boba Fett uses them individually for most purposes, using several together to create a safe anti-security field for secret forced entries.

Boot spikes (spring-loaded)

Fragmentation housing

Ripper launch tip

Cycle wave ripper

For major demolition jobs, Boba Fett is known to use an antiquated multi-detonator, less susceptible to damper shield effects than a conventional thermal detonator, and capable of tearing a starship engine into fragments.

MULTI-DETONATOR

Bounty Hunters

THE RESTRICTIVE RULE of the Empire has made criminals of many, encouraging black-market smugglers and creating long blacklists of proscribed citizens of every kind. Imperial rewards posted for all such "enemies of the state" have made bounty hunting a thriving profession. Often criminal refuse themselves, many bounty hunters act in murderous and violent ways with the sanction of Imperial law. A few work with the legitimate intention of capturing criminals, but the profession as a whole is distinguished by outstanding slime.

Head sensors allow IG-88 to see in all directions at once

Heat sensor

Poison gas packet

Motion sensor

Targeting sight

Activation filament

Magnetic sensor

Broadband antenna

Sound sensor

Vocoder

Pneumatic arms

Gas discharge valve

IG-88'S TRION GAS DISPENSER

Ammunition bandolier

Flamethrower

Sonic stunner

"Butcher" vibro-blade

Explosive core

An IG-88 droid tracked *Slave I* to Cloud City, intending to kill Boba Fett. Fett ambushed it in the scrap processing levels. He paralyzed it with an ion cannon, then finished it off, leaving the hulk for recycling.

Pulse cannon

Ammo packets

IG-88'S CONCUSSION DISCS

Worn due to use

IG-88

IG-88'S BLADE EXTENSION SET

This hideous assassin droid is one of a set of five identical robots which massacred their constructors moments after activation, and escaped their laboratories to stalk the galaxy. IG-88's incompletely formed identity leaves it obsessed with hunting and killing. Assassin droids are always hard to control and have long been illegal for good reason, since they pose a threat to any and all around them.

Neural inhibitor projectile launcher

Blast armor

Acid-proof servo wires

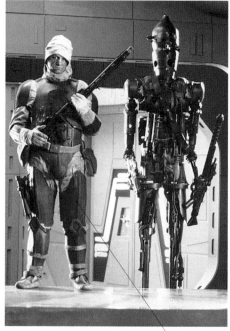

Dengar

Dengar

Trained as an Imperial assassin, Dengar underwent brain surgery that replaced his hypothalamus with circuitry, making him a nearly unfeeling killer. Now independent as a bounty hunter, he has claimed 23 bounties and carries a personal grudge against Han Solo for severe head injuries he suffered racing him through the crystal swamps of Agrilat long ago.

Poison-tipped needles

Firing chamber

Silencer tube

Release valve

Needle Barrel

IG-88'S NEEDLE DART GUN

DATA FILE

◆ IG-88 droids have attacked Boba Fett several times, badly damaging *Slave I* but never claiming Fett himself. Fett has now destroyed three of the assassin droids.

◆ Rodians like Greedo come from a culture that favors bounty hunting as a sport, though Greedo found his match in Han Solo.

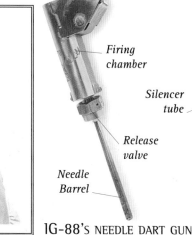

4-LOM

Once a sophisticated protocol droid made to resemble the species it worked with, 4-LOM's programming degraded and it became a criminal, specializing in anticipating the moves of target beings. Teamed with the findsman Zuckuss, 4-LOM provides information and analysis to support his partner's mysterious ways.

4-LOM   Zuckuss

Zuckuss

The bounty hunter Zuckuss uses the mystic religious rituals of findsman traditions dating back centuries on his gaseous homeworld of Gand. His uncanny abilities make other bounty hunters uneasy. Zuckuss is a tireless tracker and weirdly effective.

Targeting laser

Vision-plus scanner

Speech scrambler

Body suit

Impact armor

Chest-mounted comlink

Audio pickup and broadband antenna

Glove spikes

Activation panel and timer settings

Plasmic core

Bandolier

Projectile detonator

Ogygian cloak

Ubese clan belt-clasp

Fragmentation shell

Ammo pouches

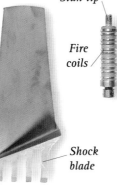

BOUSHH'S THERMAL DETONATOR

Stun tip

Fire coils

Shock blade

BOUSHH'S LANCE BLADE AND STUN ATTACHMENTS

Boushh

In a galaxy with so many bizarre creatures acting as bounty hunters (or claiming to be), it was easy for Princess Leia to adopt a convincing identity as a Ubese tracker, disguising herself with a dead hunter's helmet and garb. Leia's military training served her well as Boushh, and only Jabba suspected her real identity.

Jabba the Hutt's palace frequently brings bounty hunters together as the Hutt posts rewards for both captures and kills on a regular basis.

Shata leather pants

Traditional Ubese boots

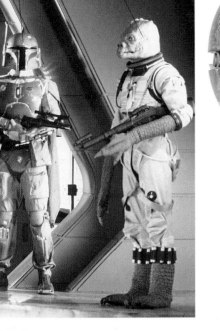

Boba Fett   Bossk

Bossk

A reptilian Trandoshan, the tough and resilient Bossk has gone from tracking runaway slaves to claiming bounties posted by the Empire – a count of 12 captures so far. Trandoshans can regenerate lost skin, fingers, and even limbs until they reach adulthood as Bossk finally has. Fond of skinning his quarry when possible, he is as vile and mean as bounty hunters get.

Warrior spines

Head bandages

Eye protection
lenses

Breath filter

Moisture
trap

Sand People
TUSKEN RAIDERS

FIERCE NOMADS OF TATOOINE, the Sand People or Tusken Raiders prowl areas like the Dune Sea and the Jundland Wastes, blending invisibly into the landscape. Masters of the desert, they survive where no one else can, protected from the suns by heavy clothing. Their savage and violent ways pit them against the moisture farmers and settlers in lonely, remote lands. They usually stay away from towns and cities, but in the dead of hot season, Raiders emerge from the wastes after the twin suns set to scavenge or steal from the edges of settlement zones. It is best to lock up tight at night – Sand People almost never come into a house but they will slay a lone resister outside.

Poisoned blade

Banthas

Banthas roam the dunes and wastes of Tatooine in herds. Sand People use these giant beasts to carry both riders and gear, forming close bonds with them, and even making them members of their clans. Sand People ride in single file to hide their numbers.

Gaderffi
stick

Thick desert
cloak

Sand
gloves

BLOODLETTING BLADE
Tusken Raider clan rituals may involve the sacrifice of animals, captives, or even condemned Sand People.

Rare water wells in canyons like Gafsa are sacred to the Tusken Raiders. Merely trespassing near one can provoke immediate violence. Intruders may be taken alive for sacrifice.

DATA FILE

◆ Tusken Raiders scavenge metal from wrecks to make their traditional terror weapon, the gaderffi (or gaffi) stick.

◆ While Sand People are nomadic, clans often have a particular cave or hollow where they gather to hold special ceremonies or to bury their dead.

Bandaged feet

Jawas

CONCEALED in dark robes that protect them from the twin suns, the timid and acquisitive Jawas scavenge scrap metal, lost droids, and equipment from refuse or the many crashed spaceships that dot the desert landscapes of Tatooine. Their glowing eyes help them see in the dark crevices where they hide, and their rodent-like faces are remarkably ugly. While there are a few Jawa settlements, most Jawas patrol the dunes and dusty rocks in gigantic sandcrawlers, ancient vehicles from a mining era long ago. Jawas can offer real bargains in the junk that they repair, but are notoriously tricky and will swindle the unwary buyer.

Droids that wander off or get thrown out as junk are favorite targets for the Jawas. Jawas always carry restraining bolts which they install to claim itinerant droids. A magnetic suction tube draws captured droids into the bowels of a roving sandcrawler.

Scoured and rusted from countless sandstorms and the blistering suns, sandcrawlers hold droid prisons, mineral ore and metal processors, and wrecked or salvaged junk of every kind.

Ionized gas filament compartment

ION POWER CHARGE CELL

Charge cell housing

Ion regulators

Primary ion accelerator

Blast nozzle

Overload breakers

Ion accelerator brace

Power transformer

IONIZATION BLASTER

Trigger

Stock

Power coupling

Mounting brace

Tread energizer

Neutral polarity node

Linkage pins

Mark II reactor drone magfield sensor ball

Contact cage

Transmitter calls or halts a droid

Droid signal receiver

Setting adjust

Belt ring

Activator

Power cell

DROID CALLER

DROID PARTS

Jawa recycling talents are legendary. If a droid is too battered even for Jawas to repair, it is cannibalized for spare parts (above). New owners who open up a droid bought from Jawas may find internal parts of which its makers never dreamed.

Heavy cloaks protect from sun glare

Bandolier

Droid caller

Glowing eyes

Ionization charge (inside belt pouch)

Tool belt

Mini-ionization pistol

Ewoks

DEEP WITHIN the primeval forests of the emerald moon of Endor, the small, furry Ewoks live in harmony with the natural world around them. They build their villages high in the oldest trees, connecting their dwellings with wooden bridges and suspended platforms. Ewoks hunt and gather by day on the forest floor, retreating to their aerial villages by night, when the forest becomes too dangerous for them.

Sounding sticks

Retaining strap

Stone knife

Leather strap

HUNTING KNIFE

Handle

Sheath

CHURI BIRD CALLERS

Churi feathers

Gurreck skull headress

Stone club head

Authority stick

Striped pelt

Hood

Teebo

A watcher of the stars and a poet at heart, Teebo has a mystical alignment with the forces of nature. His subtle perception lets him see more than meets his dreamer's eye, but he is also a practical thinker. His sound judgment has led to his position as a leader within his tribe.

Spear

Thick fur

Wicket W. Warrick

A young loner, Wicket is off traveling when he encounters Princess Leia Organa in the forest. Helping her to the relative safety of his village, he comes to trust her and senses her goodness of spirit. When Leia's friends arrive, Wicket argues that they should be spared any abuse, but his solitary habits leave him with small influence amongst the village elders. Wicket's thorough knowledge of the forest terrain greatly assists the Rebels in their later attack on the Imperial forces.

Thickened head lends weight to blows

FIGHTING CLUBS

Talisman bag

An Ewok shaman builds a collection of many magical objects and medicinal cures for his work. A spirit staff helps summon dead ancestors for assistance, while the sick or injured are touched with a powerful healing wand. The forest vegetation offers many medicinal plants, which are kept with charms in a talisman bag.

Healing wand

SHAMAN'S KIT

SHAMAN'S GHOST RATTLE

Logray

A tribal shaman and medicine man, Logray uses his knowledge of ritual and magic to help and awe his people. He still favors the old traditions of initiation and live sacrifice. The trophies on his staff of power include the remnants of old enemies. Logray is suspicious of all outsiders, an attitude reinforced by the arrival of Imperial forces.

Chief Chirpa

Leader of his tribe for 42 seasons, Chief Chirpa has the wisdom of long years. He leads his people with understanding, even though he has become a bit forgetful in his old age. His authority commits the Ewoks to their dangerous fight against the Empire.

Hood

Hunting knife

Churi skull

Staff of power

Trophy spine

Chief's medallion

Medicine bag

Striped fur

DATA FILE

◆ While their technology is primitive, the Ewoks display resourceful ingenuity, constructing hang gliders and complex traps for Imperial occupation forces.

◆ Ewoks often wear the teeth, horns, and skulls of animals they have hunted as trophies.

The Cantina Crowd

THE MOS EISLEY SPACEPORT sees a wide variety of unusual people and things, but the Mos Eisley Cantina is known as the haunt of the weirdest clientele in town. Hardened professional spacers and bizarre outlanders from distant corners of the galaxy can be found here. It's no place for the squeamish, but for its regulars, the cantina provides a pan-galactic atmosphere that helps distract them from their various misfortunes and the miserable hole of Mos Eisley. The regular band suits many tastes, and as long as foolish outsiders don't step in and get their heads blown off, everyone can have their own version of a good time. Deals get made, things get drunk, and the wrong sorts of business go the right sorts of ways. The bartender maintains a semblance of order by threatening to poison the drinks of creatures that give him trouble.

An entrance vestibule serves as a buffer between the intolerable heat outdoors and the relative cool inside the cantina. It also gives those inside an opportunity to look over new arrivals before they step in.

Seats for waiting

Droid detector

Drink cups indicate cantina's services

Mouthpiece

Farra slots

Ommni wheel

FANFAR

Hrchek Kal Fas is a tough Saurin droid trader who wisely keeps his bodyguard nearby in the cantina.

Duros are a species long adapted to space travel, with natural piloting and navigation skills. These two make regular deep space runs connecting through Mos Eisley.

Distinctive Devaronian horns

This Devaronian hides under the assumed name of Labria, on the run from a wicked past and one of the galaxy's highest bounties for his deadly crimes.

OMMNI BOX

Sound projector

Power unit

Support post

Bwom pedal

Thwee pedal

DATA FILE

◆ When Luke and Ben left the cantina they did not realize that they were spotted by the insect-eating Garindan, a low-life informant carrying an Imperial comlink.

◆ Bodies or severed limbs from altercations in the cantina never seem to be there when the authorities show up ... no one is quite sure what happens to them.

TECH MOR   TEDN D'HAI

Living beneath Mos Eisley in abandoned tunnels, this Talz named Muftak works as a pickpocket. Talz are a primitive species who use few tools, and are taken into space only by slavers.

Day vision eyes (night vision eyes beneath)

The cantina's diverse selection of legal and illegal drinks draws unusual visitors. Lamproids and other marginal species are served blood mixes of questionable origin.

Figrin D'an and his Band

The Bith musicians most often heard in the cantina are highly intelligent creatures with sophisticated musical abilities – a band called the Modal Nodes. Even though they complain, the band members enjoy their out-of-the-way dive and are glad to be away from their home world of Clak'dor VII. The lead player is an expert gambler who lives well and pays off his occasional debts with his tunes, and meanwhile tries to keep his members out of trouble. They've been asked to play at Jabba's palace, but they're too smart for that.

Enlarged cranium

Mouth tube

KLOO HORN

Large eyes

Tone mode selectors

Respiratory folds

BANDFILL

Band jacket

FIZZ (OR DOREMIAN BESHNIQUEL)

Reciprocator horns

Ploong sounder

Peel rod

Peel rods

Power indicator

Band pants

Travel boots

FIGRIN D'AN

NALAN CHEEL

DOIKK NATS

The ghastly toothed sand creatures of Tatooine's deep deserts can grow to over 100 meters in length.

Creatures

COUNTLESS VARIETIES of life forms inhabit the galaxy, many known only to those who have encountered them and myriads unclassified by galactic science. Long after dark, space pilots may trade tales over drinks about weird and horrible creatures on remote planets or in the far reaches of space. More than once these stories have turned out to be true, from the haunting howls of Hoth's stalking snow beast to the impossibly gigantic asteroid lurkers, closing their maws on fleeing starships. The doubtful traveler is often the last one to realize that a tentacle is already curled around his leg, about to draw him to some unspeakable death. In a galaxy full of creatures such as these, it pays to be careful.

Space Slug

Silicon-based space slugs survive in a vacuum, digesting minerals with a uranium-based metabolism. Recently a titan space slug was documented by an Imperial Star Destroyer on a pursuit mission in an asteroid field. The slug attacked and digested part of the Imperial vessel before being subdued.

Dianoga

Dianogas (or garbage squids) have spread throughout the galaxy, growing up to ten meters long and thriving especially in sewers. Feeding on refuse, these creatures are sometimes bred in space stations for waste processing. Older specimens are very aggressive, seizing prey in their seven muscular tentacles.

Space-living silicon-based parasites, mynocks attack the signal emitters and power cables of starships, feeding on the energy emissions. They can cause significant damage to ships they infest.

Mild-tempered rontos are used by settled Jawa clans on Tatooine as pack animals, bringing goods to cities for trade.

Tauntaun bones

Curving horns

Fanged maw

The worrt inhabits the wastelands of Tatooine, attacking almost any moving object. Jabba keeps worrts in the grounds outside his palace.

Manacles

Camouflaging white pelt

Thick insulating fur

Wampa

Standing three meters high, huge wampa ice creatures hunt tauntauns and other creatures on the snow plains of Hoth, where their howling wails blend with the icy winds at night. Cunning predators, wampas are normally solitary beasts, but they have been known to band together with uncanny intelligence in the face of threats like human settlements.

The rock wart of Tatooine uses a painful neurotoxic venom in its bite and sting to kill even large prey.

Rancor Monster

Standing five meters tall, this fearsome carnivore possesses an armored skin and colossal strength. Jabba keeps this beast in a pit beneath one of his palace courts, feeding it a live diet of unfortunate victims and watching its attacks for amusement. Jabba keeps the origin of his bizzare, freakish pet a mystery, though there are little-known legends of rancor-like monsters on the remote planet of Dathomir.

DATA FILE

◆ Dianogas change color to match their last meal, turning translucent if they have not eaten for a long time.

◆ Jabba's pet Hoover (below) looks harmless, but creeps up on sleeping victims to suck their blood at night, using its nose trunk to slither through clothing or around blankets.

Powerful jaw muscles

The animal handler Malakili became an outlaw when some of his circus beasts escaped during a show and killed much of the audience. Jabba then hired him as keeper of the murderous rancor, which Malakili has grown fond of.

Digestive spittle

Gaffi stick; gift from some Tusken Raiders for killing a giant mutant womp rat that took over their clan cave

Claws

Old circus pants

Long reaching arms

Wide grasp

Clutching fingers

Short legs

Tough, rigid hide can absorb blaster bolts

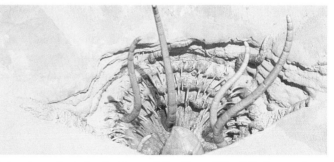

Lying in wait at the bottom of the Great Pit of Carkoon, the Sarlacc seizes its prey with lashing tentacles, drawing them into its maw, "from which none emerge." The Sarlacc slowly digests its victims over hundreds of years, merging with their metabolisms and keeping them alive to feed off their tortured consciousness – the closest the Sarlacc can come to companionship.

Stubby hooves

Droids

MECHANICAL DROIDS perform thousands of different servant functions, saving labor, doing precise or dangerous work, and taking as many different forms as there are tasks. Their abilities to think and communicate vary, from protocol droids designed to blend in with civilized society to utility droids that cannot communicate directly with humans. Droids are regarded as slaves and third-class citizens, held in contempt by those many who "don't like machinery that talks back." Those who give them a little respect can find that some droids have personalities and identities of their own.

Remote communications antenna

Photoreceptors made to look like Stacchati eyes

Stereo vocoder with sounding box

DATA FILE

◆ Most droids have their memory banks periodically erased, which prevents them from developing personalities.

◆ The agromech droid R5-D4 "Red" blew his motivator so Owen Lars would have to take R2 instead.

Old-model heavy arm plating

Decorative chest plate

Human-style manipulator hands

Standard protocol/ secretary droid legs

Jawas try to sell anything they can, prompting them to offer even this ancient droid R1-G4 to Owen Lars. A reactor drone such as this old droid would be at home in the engine room of a large starship, but would have little to do on a moisture farm.

Extensible neck strut

Manipulator arm

Binocular fine-focus vision

Photoreceptor movement servo

Reinforced body brace

Secondary manipulator arm

WED-15-77

Capable of accomplishing very specific tasks with close supervision, this binocular Treadwell has a frustratingly small independent thought processor. It assists Luke on his uncle's vaporators but prefers working for Aunt Beru since she always asks it to do the same predictable jobs.

Equipment test arm

Rotation unit

Logic housing

Communications antenna

Treads

CZ-1

This very old secretary droid was modified from a standard model to resemble the Stacchati species he once served. Abandoned on Tatooine and separated from his twin unit CZ-3 after a crash, CZ-1 broke down in the desert and was captured by Jawas. Presently his locomotors are sand-encrusted and too damaged for him to walk or move properly. Still optimistic, he hopes to be repaired and sold soon.

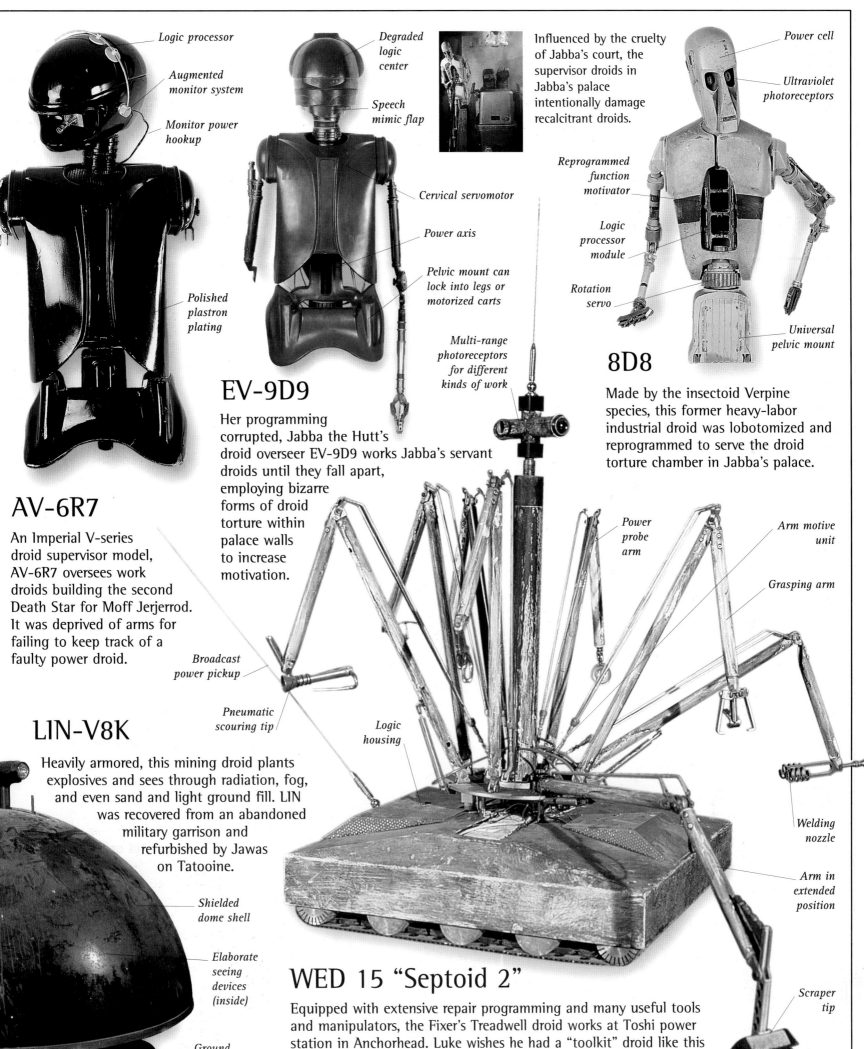

Logic processor

Augmented monitor system

Monitor power hookup

Polished plastron plating

AV-6R7

An Imperial V-series droid supervisor model, AV-6R7 oversees work droids building the second Death Star for Moff Jerjerrod. It was deprived of arms for failing to keep track of a faulty power droid.

LIN-V8K

Heavily armored, this mining droid plants explosives and sees through radiation, fog, and even sand and light ground fill. LIN was recovered from an abandoned military garrison and refurbished by Jawas on Tatooine.

Shielded dome shell

Elaborate seeing devices (inside)

Ground sensor

Degraded logic center

Speech mimic flap

Cervical servomotor

Power axis

Pelvic mount can lock into legs or motorized carts

Multi-range photoreceptors for different kinds of work

EV-9D9

Her programming corrupted, Jabba the Hutt's droid overseer EV-9D9 works Jabba's servant droids until they fall apart, employing bizarre forms of droid torture within palace walls to increase motivation.

Influenced by the cruelty of Jabba's court, the supervisor droids in Jabba's palace intentionally damage recalcitrant droids.

Power cell

Ultraviolet photoreceptors

Reprogrammed function motivator

Logic processor module

Rotation servo

Universal pelvic mount

8D8

Made by the insectoid Verpine species, this former heavy-labor industrial droid was lobotomized and reprogrammed to serve the droid torture chamber in Jabba's palace.

Power probe arm

Arm motive unit

Grasping arm

Broadcast power pickup

Pneumatic scouring tip

Logic housing

Welding nozzle

Arm in extended position

Scraper tip

WED 15 "Septoid 2"

Equipped with extensive repair programming and many useful tools and manipulators, the Fixer's Treadwell droid works at Toshi power station in Anchorhead. Luke wishes he had a "toolkit" droid like this to help him instead of his limited-function binocular Treadwell.

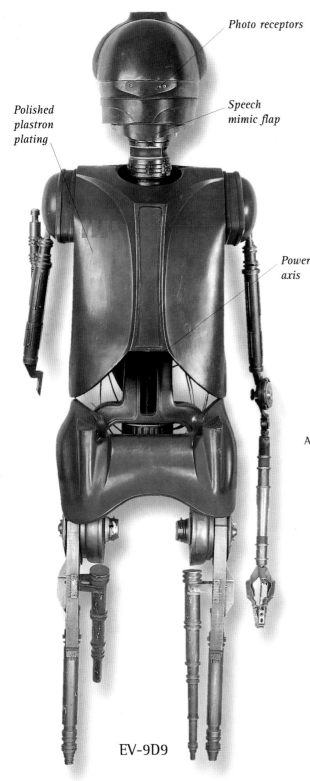

Photo receptors

Speech
mimic flap

Polished
plastron
plating

Power
axis

EV-9D9

DK

A DK PUBLISHING BOOK

PROJECT ART EDITOR Iain Morris
PROJECT EDITOR David Pickering
US EDITOR Jane Mason
MANAGING ART EDITOR Cathy Tincknell
DTP DESIGNER Kim Browne
PRODUCTION Louise Barrett, Katy Holmes, & Steve Lang
US ARCHIVIST Paloma Añoveros
US PICTURE RESEARCH Cara Evangelista
US PHOTO LIBRARY Halina Krukowski & Tina Mills

First American Edition, 1998
4 6 8 10 9 7 5 3
Published in the United States by
DK Publishing, Inc.
95 Madison Avenue
New York, New York 10016

Library of Congress Cataloging-in-Publication Data
Reynolds, David West.
Star Wars: The visual dictionary / by David West Reynolds. — 1st American ed.
        p.   cm.
Includes index.
ISBN 0-7894-3481-4
1. Star Wars films—Dictionaries—Juvenile literature.
2. Star Wars films—Pictorial works—Juvenile literature.   I. Title
        PN1995.9.S695R49   1998
791.43'75—dc21   98-22877
                                                        CIP

Color reproduction in the United Kingdom by DOT Gradations
Printed in Italy by A. Mondadori Editore, Verona

Acknowledgements

The author and DK Publishing would like to extend special thanks to the people who helped this project come together: Paloma Añoveros, Curator of the Lucasfilm Archives, allowed us many more photography sessions than originally planned, and helped at every round to bring out obscure original props wherever possible and restore great pieces to their proper appearance. Her support made many of the most interesting photos in this book possible. Gillian Libbert, Character Appearances Coordinator at Lucasfilm, gave us her professional skills to supervise special new photos of Boba Fett and Darth Vader. Cara Evangelista, Lucasfilm Licensing Division's Publishing Coordinator, worked through an unending stream of demanding image requests with unfailing charm to deliver the variety and quality we needed. Don Post of Don Post Studios provided a close look at some of Boba Fett's more obscure weaponry with new fabrications from his remarkable life-size bounty hunter replica. Mathew Clayson of Hi-Impact Productions created and generously loaned several pieces of stormtrooper gear to the project. Other new fabrications were made by Ann Marie Reynolds, the author,

and Edward Endres of Fyberdyne Laboratories. Anna Bies recreated the cantina band uniform and kept the costumes looking their best during the shoot for the momentous Modal Node reunion. Fon Davis and Mark Buck of ILM helped out on that gig by playing the fizz and bandfill respectively. Marc Wendt in the Lucasfilm Product Archives faithfully dispatched lightsaber replicas to our front lines when some of the Jedi would have been without weapons. Steve Sansweet's grand Star Wars Encyclopedia, in pre-publication form, was a trusty and well-written resource, an especially welcome ally in the research for this project. Finally and most instrumentally, there was a crack team of pros at the top: US Editor Jane Mason oversaw this project through blizzards of approvals shipments and stood as our champion of clear text; Project Art Editor Iain Morris gave the book its visual structure and shaped its content with his design and image selections, always finding ways to "make it cooler," while Project Editor David Pickering made all the text possible with his vital encouragement and editorial guidance. Lucas Licensing Director of Publishing Lucy Wilson gave the lot the chance to

make this book a reality, and we hope she enjoys it as much as we did. Thanks!

DK Publishing would also like to thank:
Giles Keyte for additional photography at Leavesden Studios, England; Nelson Hall for additional photography at Skywalker Ranch, California; Kristin Ward and Will Lach for additional editorial work in New York; Nick Turpin for editorial assistance; Anne Sharples and Peter Fickling for design assistance; Helen Stallion for additional picture research in the UK.

Additional picture credits
t=top b=bottom c=center l=left r=right
Colin Keates (Natural History Museum)/Andreas Ensiedal: 25cr, 46tcr;
Wallace Collection/Geoff Dann: 46tcl;
Geoff Dann/Dave Rudkin/Tim Ridley/Bruce Chisholm 46tcl;
Martin Norris 25c